Castle in the Sky:

George Whittell Jr. and the Thunderbird Lodge

Second Edition

Ronald M. and Susan A. James

ISBN-10: 0-9718047-1-0

ISBN-13: 978-0-9718047-1-5

Library of Congress Control Number: 2005904158

Interior and Cover Design by Caren Parnes, ENTERPRISING GRAPHICS, Windsor, CA

Edited by Rose Marie Cleese, RMC CREATIVE, San Mateo, CA

Printed in the United States of America

Cover photography and photographs on the copyright page and opposite the Table of Contents courtesy of Vance Fox. Photograph on the Table of Contents page courtesy of Scott Klette.

The Special Collections Department of the University of Nevada, Reno, Library, provided many of the historic photographs in this volume.

Photographic attributions appear within the book's photo captions. Where no attribution appears, photographs are courtesy of the Thunderbird Lodge Collection or Special Collections.

The Second Edition was funded in part by a generous grant from the Robert Z. Hawkins Foundation.

Thunderbird Lodge Preservation Society
P.O. Box 6812, Lake Tahoe, NV 89450

The Thunderbird Lodge Preservation Society (TLPS), a 501(c)(3) non-profit organization, is responsible for the preservation and interpretation of the estate.

This book is dedicated to Father Donald Mason

1924–1986

Before he became a Jesuit priest, Donald Mason worked for George Whittell at the Thunderbird Lodge during the summers of 1941 and 1942. As the son of George's trusted personal physician, he was allowed rare glimpses into the private world of a reclusive man.

I met Father Mason in 1983 when he returned to the Thunderbird Lodge where he sat on the balcony sharing all the wonderful stories of his experiences with Captain Whittell and his *Thunderbird* boat there at the "Castle in the Sky." This chance meeting was the start of an enduring friendship that continues in spirit. Father Mason's vivid recollections made a lasting impression, convincing me that preservation of the Thunderbird Lodge should be fulfilled.

Joan Gibb
Board of Directors
Thunderbird Lodge Preservation Society

Table of Contents

Called Captain after a rank he acquired during World War I, George Whittell, Jr., was one of the world's most eligible bachelors until his conduct shocked acceptable society.

HE WAS KNOWN AS ONE OF THE WEST COAST'S MOST ENIGMATIC RESIDENTS. GEORGE WHITTELL, JR., WAS BORN IN 1881 IN SAN FRANCISCO, THE CHILD OF AN ECONOMIC ELITE MADE RICH BY THE CALIFORNIA GOLD RUSH. A TEENAGER IN 1900, HE WAS POSITIONED TO ENJOY THE EXCITEMENT OF A DYNAMIC REGION AND NEW CENTURY. FABULOUSLY WEALTHY, IMPULSIVE, AND CAPRICIOUS, A YOUTHFUL WHITTELL BARRELED THROUGH LIFE AT FULL-THROTTLE, COLLECTING EXOTIC ANIMALS, ELEGANT AUTOMOBILES AND BOATS, BEAUTIFUL WOMEN, AND CONTENTIOUS LAWSUITS ALONG THE WAY. HE WAS ONE OF THE MORE NOTORIOUS PLAYBOYS OF CALIFORNIA AND NEVADA, INDULGING IN A SUCCESSION OF MARRIAGES AND LIAISONS THAT FUELED THE REGION'S GOSSIP MILLS. A RECLUSE IN HIS LATER YEARS, WHITTELL SHUNNED PUBLICITY, AND, IN DOING SO, INSPIRED SPECULATION ABOUT HIS EVERY MOVE. BY THE TIME OF HIS DEATH IN 1969, HE HAD BECOME THE STUFF OF LEGEND.

Whittell received a European education, claiming fluency in seven languages. A hedonist with near-infinite resources, he was committed to the idea of never working, a goal he realized to the best of his ability throughout his life. His story would ultimately include a sojourn with Barnum & Bailey's Circus, and adventures in the midst of combat during World War I, as well as a fascination for technology and the fastest cars, planes, and boats.

Sleek and beautiful, Whittell's Thunderbird *cut through the waters of Lake Tahoe and became one of the great wooden speedboats of the twentieth century.*

Opposite Page: Whittell built his Tahoe estate as a mountain retreat affording the best of comfort and view.

It would be easy to dismiss George Whittell, Jr., as a historical footnote, a son of wealth who did little to enhance the reputation of his class. Of slight importance is the fact that he tinkered with auto design and was captivated with the Duesenberg, one of the most luxurious vehicles of the early twentieth century. Similarly, Whittell knew all the rich and famous of his time, ranging from boxing heavyweight Jack Dempsey and actress Irene Rich to that well-known fixture of the 1930s, adventurer Frank "Bring 'Em Back Alive" Buck. Yet, all of this together would hardly cause the historical spotlight to shine on him for more than a fleeting moment.

In spite of Whittell's dedication to idleness, he left a remarkable inheritance for others to enjoy. Because of a seemingly insignificant twist in a real estate transaction, the multimillionaire turned his

Whittell purchased an unprecedented six Duesenbergs, a handmade luxury vehicle, of which the total number produced was barely 1,000. (Courtesy of Automobile Quarterly)

attention to Lake Tahoe in the 1930s. He built one of the nation's finest retreats, the Thunderbird Lodge, on the east shore of this stunning location, and he tied up nearly a third of the lake's acreage, keeping development at bay. It was his legacy, even if he had not intended to hand it to posterity.

Whittell's story is more than a tale of affluence and privilege without direction. His castle and the vast stretches of undeveloped land in the Tahoe Basin remain as the vestiges of his wealth. This, then, is a portrait of that man and what he left behind.

Much of Lake Tahoe's Nevada shoreline remains pristine, thanks to Whittell's reluctance to develop his property. (Courtesy of Ron James)

Opposite Page: The Thunderbird Lodge, arguably Whittell's greatest achievement, now a public legacy open for tours and special events. (Courtesy of Scott Klette)

THE CALIFORNIA GOLD RUSH OF 1849 CAPTURED THE IMAGINATION OF THE WORLD, AS IT DOES TO THIS DAY, WITH ITS FABULOUS WEALTH AND OPPORTUNITY. HUNDREDS OF THOUSANDS OF GOLD SEEKERS STREAMED TO THE PACIFIC COAST, HOPING TO "STRIKE IT RICH." AMBITION COULD TURN ONE'S FORTUNES FROM POVERTY TO AFFLUENCE, BUT THE VAST MAJORITY OF THOSE INTREPID ARGONAUTS DID LITTLE MORE THAN LEAVE BROKEN, RICHER ONLY IN EXPERIENCE. NONETHELESS, CALIFORNIA'S GOLD DID CREATE A REORDERING OF SOCIETY, GIVING BIRTH TO A NEW ARISTOCRACY. TALENT AND THE LUCK OF THE DRAW IMPARTED STATUS TO A FEW WHO ROSE TO COMMAND THE PINNACLE OF THIS YOUNG WEST. ARRIVING WITH SOME CAPITAL ON HAND, OF COURSE, ENHANCED ONE'S CHANCES FOR SUCCESS.[1]

OUTGOING   AND   INCOMING.

The mining West promised wealth but rarely delivered. For most, fortune turned for the worse as suggested by artist, writer, and humorist J. Ross Browne. (Courtesy of the Nevada Historical Society)

Opposite Page: Whittell grew up in one of the largest, most cosmopolitan cities of the West. Wealth and position allowed him to turn San Francisco into his private playground. (Courtesy of the San Francisco History Center, San Francisco Public Library)

George Whittell's two immigrant grandfathers shrewdly exploited Gold Rush opportunities, laying the foundation for a financial empire. Hugh B. Whittell was born in Tyrone, Ireland, in 1811, immigrating to America in 1828. He traveled a great deal and eventually settled in New York where he worked as a clothing importer. Maternal grandfather Nicholas B. Luning was born in 1822 in the German-speaking port of Hamburg. His was a family of merchants and bankers. At twenty, he sailed for New York, but he did not linger on the East Coast for long.[2]

The two men, first Whittell and then Luning, felt the lure of gold in California. Both arrived in 1849, and they quickly tapped into the vibrant economy. Prices were inflated and the flow of gold charged the air itself with fantastic vigor. An experienced entrepreneur, Hugh Whittell made a small fortune investing in mining claims and buying real estate throughout San Francisco's Bay Area.[3]

Luning arrived a few months after the initial excitement. Having enough money at his disposal—about $6,000—to open a small bank, he specialized in loans to merchants facing financial emergencies. His business succeeded remarkably, and he was soon widely invested in Bay Area real estate. Luning helped found the San Francisco Water Company and the precursor of the Pacific Gas and Electric Company. By the time of his death in 1890, the sixty-eight-year-old businessman had an estimated worth of about $29,000,000.[4]

The fabulous Whittell–Luning fortunes melded together in 1879 when one of Luning's daughters, Anna, married George Whittell, Sr., himself heir to Hugh Whittell's solid financial bedrock. Upon her father's death, Anna inherited more than $9,000,000, giving her husband the means to build an even greater empire.

Young George Whittell, Sr., was a dashing entrepreneur and the son of wealth with roots in the California Gold Rush of 1849.

Anna Luning was heir to a fortune. Her father, Nicolas Luning, had built a West Coast empire exploiting the opportunities of the California Gold Rush.

Ambition, talent, and the backing of extraordinary wealth made Whittell, Sr., one of the foremost businessmen on the West Coast. Through shrewd investments and cut-throat business management, he became a giant among the economic greats.[5]

On September 28, 1881, Anna gave birth to twins, George, Jr., and Nicholas. When diphtheria claimed Nicholas's life in 1885, George became the sole heir of millions. Lacking a competing successor, Junior, as his family called him, grew up like a prince, knowing that he alone would inherit the kingdom. A baby named Albert Whittell, suspiciously brought home in 1892 to be raised as a foster child, did little to shake George's confidence that one day he would claim his family's immense fortune.[6] This circumstance did not escape wealthy West Coast parents of eligible daughters. The fact that the boy turned into a handsome redheaded man with an imposing six-foot-four frame only enhanced his appeal. The stage was set for the next chapter of the epic unfolding of a dynasty.

George Whittell, Jr., was given the best education and opportunities. Growing up, however, he focused only on the things that interested him, and the center of his attention could change on a whim. George's penchant for self-indulgence inspired him to follow many a boy's dream of running away to the circus. As a teenager, he spent time with Barnum & Bailey's Circus, where he developed a lifelong love of wild animals. After his stint under the big top, Whittell returned to his parents' home, but it was clear that this heir would not follow the conventions of his powerful lineage.[7]

Like the new century, the young Whittell was brash yet full of promise. The cigarette did not acquire widespread popularity in America until World War I.

George Whittell, Jr., loved animals and speed. Horseback riding was an obvious indulgence.

Affluent parents invested hope in the successor to their fortune. Growing up, Junior wanted for nothing.

Whittell's love of technology and his unlimited wealth enabled him to be a cutting-edge consumer of automobiles. Here, the young daredevil and a friend show off an early turn-of-the-century car.

A speedboat gave young Whittell the freedom to gain complete command of his world. Junior is shown here racing around Lake Como, Italy.

Part of Whittell's early experience included time in Europe, a parental attempt to civilize the beast. Junior possessed an ability to learn languages quickly, but he encountered nothing that changed his general attitude of indolence. He had wealth at his disposal, and he was determined to exploit every chance for having fun to its fullest.[8]

Very early, the young man developed an aptitude for driving fast cars, squiring unsuitable women, and embarrassing his parents. In 1903, while George, Sr., and Anna tried to arrange a proper marriage for their twenty-one-year-old son, he shocked them by eloping with chorus girl Florence Boyere. Whittell, Sr., felt compelled to pay sufficient money to annul the inappropriate match, silence the bride, and clean the record. The attempt at a coverup failed. The marriage was dissolved and his son momentarily reined in, but not before the incident had exploded into a public scandal.[9]

A year later in August 1904, Boyere sued for the last $500 of her annulment. There was no adequate attempt to buy her continued silence before she made it to court. Word was clearly out. The high society of San Francisco's Bay Area was soon aware that one of the region's most eligible bachelors had decreased dramatically in marketability.

As a prospective husband, Junior had become problematic. He also managed to demonstrate poor qualities in other arenas. During the same year as his annulment, the brash playboy captured headlines with reckless driving. On the night of April 2, 1904, Whittell was speeding on an East Bay road with several friends when he crashed into a buggy. The accident destroyed his $12,000 automobile and caused serious injuries. One of the injured, Alice O'Day, sued her careless driver, and Whittell began his life-long relationship with a defendant's chair.[10]

The popularity of the British comedy, _Floradora_, featuring six beautiful young women swept across North America. The cast gave Junior ample opportunity to select the object of his next scandal. (Courtesy of Musicals101.com)

A San Francisco newspaper once referred to George Whittell, Jr., as "the King-Sized Millionaire with Tassels."

At the close of 1904, Junior once again found the love of his life. Josephine "Josie" Cunningham was a member of the Floradora Sextet, well-known stage performers. This time, the young man's insolence attracted national attention. He found the perfect bride to disappoint his parents and shock their society. George, Sr., and Anna, now veterans of damage control, immediately went to work. Before their impulsive son could elope, his beleaguered parents had him exiled with chaperones to Europe. George ducked his guardians and fled back to New Jersey where he rendezvoused with Josie. They quickly married.[11] 🌿

There was little hope of rehabilitating the image of an impetuous rogue who insisted on making a fool of himself. The elder Whittells gave in to Junior's persistence and accepted their new daughter-in-law. Within months, however, Josie filed for divorce, explaining in a letter that it was terribly difficult to live with the egocentric heir.[12] In the midst of the scandal, erroneous rumors flew around Northern California that George, Jr., was about to marry again, this time to a Miss Harrington of San Mateo. 🌿

Josie returned to the stage, but young George was not able to resume his appointed station as easily. This affluent successor to a financial empire now had little prospect of making a proper

George Whittell, Sr., expected his son to be the successor to a financial empire. Patience and prodding failed to yield returns.

The great 1906 earthquake destroyed the Whittell home at 1155 California Street on Nob Hill, in the center of San Francisco. George, Jr., captured the popular imagination when he rescued his father and family treasures during a bold escape.

Befriending San Francisco's fire and police departments gave Whittell access to special events as well as a siren and red light for his car. The above photo captures a fireman's banquet.

dynastic match. One indiscretion might be forgiven, but a pattern was clearly emerging. No parents of a suitable young woman could accept such an unabashed scoundrel. ❦

By 1906, at the age of twenty-four, George, Jr., had proven himself to be a great disappointment to his family. This year, however, witnessed one of the rare times when the young bon vivant managed to win popular praise. Reporting about the great San Francisco earthquake, newspapers noted that Whittell used his fast car to race through the debris and fires. He plucked his father and various treasures from their Nob Hill home and sped down Powell Street and the steep ruin-filled slopes of the City to the wharf. There they secured transportation to the calmer east shore of the Bay. It was a daring escape, and Junior emerged as a dashing hero.[13] The praise was short-lived. ❦

Within a few months of the disaster, Whittell made headlines again, reinforcing his negative image. This time, his father blamed Junior's excesses on a companion, the son of the Guatemalan president. Exasperated, the elder Whittell scuffled with this young man, who fell down a flight of stairs.[14] Junior's failings had infected his father who now found himself in court. Those who knew young George described him as an odd mixture of a sensitive, almost bashful, contemplative heir. Bad publicity focused on the boisterous drunk capable of doing anything at a party or behind the wheel. ❦

After the earthquake, the Whittell family shifted its chief residence to the exclusive community of Woodside, south of San Francisco near Stanford University. George, Sr., built a magnificent Renaissance Revival-style house surrounded by ample grounds to ensure privacy. Although his son was drawn to the excitement of San Francisco—and wherever else he could find it—George, Jr., called the Woodside estate home for the rest of his life. ❧

It was during this time that the young millionaire formed an unusual liaison with police and fire departments. These common guardians of society were not regarded as the proper companions for the son of aristocrats, but Whittell

The thrill-seeking Captain took his quest for speed to the air in one of the craft he dubbed "Thunderbird."

The Duesenberg would eventually realize Whittell's ideal of the ultimate driving machine, combining speed and luxury. Pictured here is Whittell's 1933 Duesenberg, a J-508 Weymann Fishtail Speedster. (Courtesy of the Robert Lee Trust)

Whittell's fascination with technology and fast living led him to become a pilot. Here, he is seen seated on the left at the controls of one of his later aircraft acquisitions.

nevertheless found friendship among their ranks. He became an Honorary Fire Marshal in San Francisco, using that title to obtain a siren and red light, which he employed inappropriately to race through the streets of the City.[15] ❧

Whittell developed a jet-set lifestyle before there were jets, traveling from one continent to another on a whim, enjoying the best in cars and all the women he could seduce. He owned those vehicles of the time that could grant him the fastest speeds and the greatest thrills. As a connoisseur of the latest technology, he was drawn to flying and became a capable pilot. ❧

Above & Top Left: World War I gave George, Jr., pictured above on the left, new experiences and friends as well as the title "Captain." Bottom Left: This autographed image is of Marshall Henri-Philippe Pétain, the hero of World War I's Battle of Verdun and later the disgraced leader of Vichy France beginning in 1940.

In 1914 at the outbreak of World War I, Whittell, now in his early thirties, could not resist the chance for excitement. He served as an ambulance driver on the Italian front before the entry of the United States into the war. He later claimed to have purchased a biplane in the early years of the war so he could volunteer for the famed Lafayette Escadrille, the American expeditionary air force.[16] It is, in fact, unlikely that the spoiled aristocrat would have submitted to the constraining daily rigors of a military pilot, but it is possible that he found an opportunity to fly an occasional mission with the unit. Whether this actually happened remains unclear in a past that Whittell purposefully made murky. Nonetheless, the story typifies the sort of mystique that Whittell developed for himself as he floated between reality and legend in order to enhance a dashing daredevil persona.

With the entry of the United States into the war in 1917, Whittell received an officer's commission. Rumors of spy missions that exploited his fluency in several languages persisted even after his death in 1969, but the truth behind the accounts is again elusive. Evidence does sur-

vive, however, of commendations he earned, and it appears that he did see combat.[17] Whittell emerged from the war with great stories and the rank of captain, a title he retained for the rest of his life as though it were a noble designation. ꕤ

Between his daring European exploits, Whittell paused long enough to fall in love with a woman his parents could accept. Parisian Elia Pascal was beautiful and possessed that air of sophistication Americans tend to ascribe to the French. The two married in 1919 and settled into a life of privilege in Woodside.[18] By all accounts happy at first, the marriage eventually withered into a loosely knit relationship that the public regarded as a sham. With continued

World War I also gave George, Jr., a marriage that, unlike the others, would last him a lifetime. Elia Pascal was a beautiful Parisian sophisticate. It was not the match his parents had planned, but it was more suitable than Junior's previous marital experiments.

Life between the Captain and Elia began as a loving, nearly conventional marriage.

By the early 1920s, Elia had settled into the role of Mrs. Whittell, a privileged spouse who enjoyed the wealth and looked the other way.

George Whittell, Sr., could do little more than hold his financial empire together for as long as he lived. There was no real hope that Junior would successfully step into his shoes.

interest in the multi-million-dollar heir, popular opinion looked at George's ongoing exploits and his peculiar marriage as grist for the gossip mills. Eventually, Elia would spend most of the year in her native Paris, but the couple remained close and never divorced. ⚜

For decades George, Sr., looked on his son as the future of the empire. Once, he gave Junior $25,000 and told him to start a business, hoping that the combination of independence and opportunity would inspire greatness. The plan proved unsuccessful. Finally, the exasperated father forced young Whittell to keep an office at the Whittell Realty Company in San Francisco, imposing a schedule and some degree of work ethic on his rebellious, self-indulgent offspring. Ultimately, that too failed.[19] ⚜

On March 26, 1922, the day his father died, Junior walked into the Whittell Realty Company and fired Eugene P. Connelly who had managed the business since 1884. He then turned over his keys to the staff and said he would not return.[20] He never did. In spite of all this, George, Sr.'s, well-crafted business carried on throughout his son's life. With the death of his father, the Captain, as he preferred to be called, rededicated himself to a life of licentious self-indulgence. Whittell became one of the richest forty-year-olds in America, having inherited millions from a father who had slaved away his entire life building a fortune.[21] ⚜

Whittell was now emancipated from the oversight and judgment of a critical parent who was a champion of American capitalism. The middle-aged Captain was rich beyond dreams and free to behave in any way he wished.

Elia was the setting for lawsuits and mutiny in response to the Captain's tyranny.

The Captain became the consummate 1920s jet-setter, collecting acquaintances among celebrities from the sporting and entertainment worlds. Boxer Jack Dempsey autographed this photograph in 1924 to "my friend."

Shortly after his father died, he flexed his new financial muscle by purchasing a 136-foot yacht, which he christened Elia.[22] The people who worked for him were, perhaps, the most frequent victims of Whittell's petulant ways. While yachting off the coast of Mexico, George threw his cook overboard for not preparing breakfast at three in the morning. The cook sued him. Three years later, Junior's abusive excesses reached a climax again, inspiring the entire crew to mutiny. The imposing veteran threw them all overboard. They, too, sued. It mattered little to the millionaire. Money was not an issue. Insubordination was never tolerated.[23]

Like a character from the pages of an F. Scott Fitzgerald novel, Whittell lived up to the reputation of the Roaring Twenties. Whatever the specifics of his experience, the existing photographs place him in exotic settings and in the company of the greatest leaders, the bravest military heroes, the most prominent aristocrats, and a galaxy of celebrities from the period.[24] The decade drew to a close, however, and for both Whittell and the nation, 1929 would prove to be pivotal.

That year, Josie, George's ex-wife, gave him a lion cub, whom he called Bill.[25] Allowed to roam freely at Woodside and later at the Thunderbird Lodge, Bill became one of the millionaire's closest friends. This was also a time when the middle-aged tycoon formed a Nevada-based business named George Whittell and Company Investments. The Silver State had become a haven for the wealthy because of its lack of income and

Above, Left & Right: Until Bill the lion came into his life, Whittell had little reason to trust those who claimed to be his friends. In this animal, the millionaire found one of his closest companions.

estate taxes. Whittell kept his mansion at Woodside, as well as his vast property holdings in San Francisco, but Northern Nevada became a second home and a means to dodge the California tax structure.[26]

Also in 1929, Whittell purchased two new Model J Duesenbergs, cutting-edge, break-the-bank luxury passenger cars suitable for racing. Whittell's quest for the fastest, most elegant mode of transportation remained from the days when he terrorized the streets of San Francisco. The Model J was an aluminum-bodied wonder touted as the perfect marriage of opulence and speed. The vehicle suited its new owner. Writing for *Automobile Quarterly* in 1988, J. M. Fenster observed, "The J-Duesenberg offered the combination of attributes most valued by Whittell, especially in the power it imparted. On paper, it was not even approached by other cars,

but on the road, it was just a car the way a crown is just a hat. ...By all means a man to impose his will on others, the implication of the Duesenberg's power would not be lost on George Whittell."[27]

Perhaps one of Whittell's greatest achievements in the world of capital occurred in 1929. In what may have been his only act of business acumen, he liquidated his stock holdings shortly before the great Wall Street collapse of that year. Whittell explained his anticipation of the Crash of 1929 to the *San Francisco Chronicle* by stating that "when men stop boozing, womanizing and gambling, the bloom is off the rose."[28] He took $50,000,000 out of a market that only a few months later would have devoured much of his wealth. Instead, he had ready cash during the Great Depression, an uncommon commodity for the time.[29]

A connoisseur of all that was fast and beautiful, Whittell found the Duesenberg perfectly suited to his tastes. Pictured here is Whittell's 1933 Duesenberg, a J-508 Weymann Fishtail Speedster. (Courtesy of Robert Lee Trust)

The Captain drove his sleek J-508 Weyman Fishtail Speedster only once, disenchanted after a friend compared it with a Holstein cow. (Courtesy of the Robert Lee Trust)

Chapter 1 Notes

[1] For a discussion of the international impact of the California Gold Rush see J. S. Holliday, *The World Rushed In: The California Gold Rush Experience* (New York: Simon and Schuster, 1981) and Holliday's more recent *Rush for Riches: Gold Fever and the Making of California* (Berkeley: University of California Press, 1999).

[2] The early days of California pioneers Hugh Whittell and Nicholas Luning are recounted in Amelia Ransome Neville's, *The Fantastic City: Memoirs of the Social and Romantic Life of Old San Francisco*, ed. Virginia Brastow (Cambridge, Massachusetts: Houghton Mifflin Co., 1932); Society of First Steamship Pioneers, *First Steamship Pioneers* (San Francisco: H. S. Crocker and Co., c. 1874); Bailey Millard, *The History of the San Francisco Bay Region* (Chicago: American Historical Society, 1924). The Thunderbird Lodge Preservation Society (TLPS) Archive includes a great deal of material on both men, mostly in the form of documents collected by various researchers.

[3] Millard, *History of the San Francisco Bay Region*, 400; "The Tycoon Who Got Away." *San Francisco Chronicle* (October 20, 1966).

[4] "Nicholas Luning Dead." *San Francisco Chronicle* (August 12, 1890).

[5] "Trying to Find Where Whittell Really Resides." *San Francisco Call* (March 16, 1900); J. M. Fenster, "The Private Universe of George Whittell." *Automobile Quarterly*, 26 (1988), 88-105. While Fenster's article focuses on George Whittell, Jr.'s, love of automobiles, particularly Duesenbergs, he also writes about the merger of the Whittell-Luning fortunes and the privileged life of George Whittell, Jr.

[6] Millard, *History of the San Francisco Bay Region*, 403; Fenster, "The Private Universe of George Whittell", 88-105. See also June Morrall, "Woodside Man Had an Ultra-Rich Lifestyle." *San Mateo County Times*, Other Times section. (TLPS Archive clipping file. Date uncertain; perhaps May 5, 2000).

[7] Fenster, "The Private Universe of George Whittell," 88-105.

[8] *Ibid.*; Morrall, "Woodside Man Had an Ultra-Rich Lifestyle." *San Mateo County Times*.

[9] Fenster, "The Private Universe of George Whittell", 88-105. The TLPS Archive includes numerous donated newspaper clippings that refer to this early marriage, but dates and names of newspapers were not preserved with the clippings.

[10] "Four Ladies Badly Hurt." *San Francisco Chronicle* (April 2, 1904); "Their Condition Very Serious." *San Francisco Chronicle* (April 3, 1904). "Automobile Accident Causes a Damage Suit." *San Francisco Call* (April 3, 1904). TLPS Archive, newspaper clippings.

[11] "George Whittell, Jr. Arrives with Bride, Josie Cunningham." *San Francisco Call* (November 17, 1904).

[12] Letter from J. Cunningham, TLPS Archive. See also undated newspaper clipping without provenience describing the divorce, TLPS Archive.

[13] "Wild Ride to Safety in an Auto." *San Francisco Call* (May 12, 1906); "The Tycoon Who Got Away." *San Francisco Chronicle* (October 20, 1966).

[14] "Son of President of Guatemala Sues for Damages from Being Thrown Downstairs While in Company of George Whittell, Jr." *San Francisco Call* (January 7, 1908).

[15] Fenster, "The Private Universe of George Whittell", 88-105; the George Whittell File at the Special Collections Department, University of Nevada, Reno Library, includes numerous certificates from Bay Area firemen and police.

[16] Tamar A. Mehuron, "The Lafayette Escadrille," *Air Force Magazine*, December 2000, 74-79.

[17] University of Nevada Special Collections Department, George Whittell File, Letters of Commendations for Service in World War I. See also Karen Barney and Bill Dohrmann, "Interview with Warren Crane, George Whittell's Personal Engineer." (October 17, 2002), TLPS Archive.

[18] Millard, *History of the San Francisco Bay Region*, 403.

[19] Recollection of John Lewis, relayed on History Day at the Thunderbird Lodge, September 3, 2000.

[20] *Ibid.*

[21] "Death Calls Pioneer San Francisco Capitalist." *San Francisco Examiner* (March 27, 1922); "Whittell's Millions Left to Relatives." *San Francisco Chronicle* (March 31, 1922).

[22] "List of Yachts of the United States and Canada, 1927," TLPS Archive.

[23] This story is recounted in "Merry Capt. Whittell's Pet Lion Plays a $200,000 Joke," *American Weekly*, 1934.

[24] Photograph collections exist in the TLPS Archive and at the Special Collections Department, University of Nevada, Reno Library.

[25] Fenster, "The Private Universe of George Whittell," 96.

[26] "One Sound State," *Nevada State Journal*, 1936, is a collection of the newspaper's articles outlining Nevada's favorable tax structure. Included is a reference to George Whittell and his Nevada land purchase. The Nevada State Archives in the Nevada Department of Cultural Affairs, has extensive records related to the incorporation of the Nevada-based George Whittell and Company, Inc.

[27] Fenster, "The Private Universe of George Whittell," 95. See also Leon Mandel, *American Cars* (New York: Stewart, Tabori and Chang, 1982), 219; Suzanne R. Stanis, et. al. "Auburn Cord Duesenberg Automobile Facility," National Historic Landmark Nomination, 2004, National Register of Historic Places, National Park Service, Washington, D.C.; Don Butler, *Auburn, Cord, Duesenberg* (Osceola, Wisconsin: Motorbooks International, 1992).

[28] "A Man's Castle: Tycoon's Tale Ends on Sorrowful Note." *North Lake Tahoe Bonanza* (October 12, 1994). This is the second article in Patrick McCartney's two-part story on George Whittell, Jr. "Inside the Whittell Castle: Eccentric Leaves Colorful Legacy at Lake Tahoe" appeared in the *Bonanza* on October 7, 1994.

[29] Close friend John Lewis described this chapter in Whittell's life. Recollection of John Lewis, relayed on History Day at the Thunderbird Lodge, September 3, 2000.

NNA LUNING WHITTELL DIED ON OCTOBER 12, 1931. SHE WAS SEVENTY-FIVE YEARS OLD. WITH THE DEATH OF HIS MOTHER, GEORGE WHITTELL, JR., FOUND HIMSELF SOLE HEIR TO AN ENORMOUS AMOUNT OF WEALTH AND FREE OF ALL PARENTAL ATTEMPTS TO INHIBIT HIS CONDUCT. TWO YEARS AFTER ANNA'S DEATH, GEORGE'S YOUNGER FOSTER BROTHER, ALFRED, CHALLENGED THE WILL OF THE ONLY MOTHER HE HAD EVER KNOWN. ALFRED HAD MADE A REMARKABLE SUCCESS OF HIMSELF, ATTENDING YALE, BECOMING AN ENGINEER, AND WORKING HARD. HE INSISTED THAT WHILE ANNA NEVER PUT IT IN WRITING, SHE MEANT FOR HER SONS TO SPLIT HER $10,000,000 ESTATE.[1]

A pleasant moment shared by Elia and foster brother Albert Whittell gives little indication of the stormy waters ahead.

Alfred initiated a protracted legal struggle that underscored an emerging theme in George's life. The Captain had been sued before, and this would not be the last time his lawyers would be called to court. In fact, a notorious case had just ended in which Evelyn Turner, an "entertainer," accused Junior of having her whipped by another woman "for his edification" at a party in 1930.[2] Whittell successfully delayed the trial until 1933, when the court awarded Turner $5,062. He lost an appeal.[3]

There were even more lawsuits. The Captain liked to socialize while in the company of Bill the lion, inspiring one incident that returned Whittell to court and the attention of the media. On New Year's Eve, 1933, the two sauntered into a hotel in Redwood City, California, where owner William B. Grosskurth alleged that Whittell "sic-ed" the lion on him. In his suit for damages, the hapless Grosskurth recounted injuries he received during a

Opposite Page: The Thunderbird Lodge, circa 1941, had assumed almost all of its present-day form within a year of its construction. In this photo, the first boathouse in the foreground, now sealed with glass block, was in the process of being converted into a swimming pool.

The lion, Bill, was one of the Captain's many non-human friends who originally resided at the Woodside estate. The two frequented bars together.

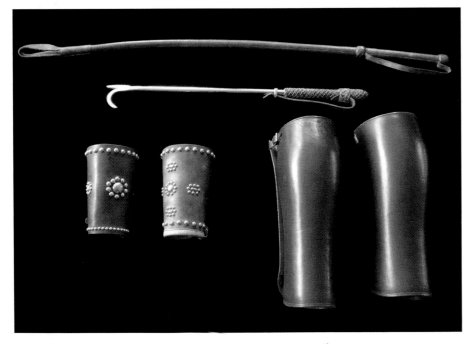

Whittell's lion taming equipment is a reminder of times spent with Bill. (Courtesy of Ron James)

game of cat and mouse, instigated by Whittell. For his part, the Captain maintained that "Kitty wouldn't hurt anyone, though occasionally he does playfully rip the coat off someone's back."[4]

Whether it was age or a growing disdain for people who seemed only to want access to his wealth, the former party-loving playboy became more and more reclusive. Whittell's increasing absence from society fueled speculation about his activities. Alfred's lawsuit added even more color.

George used whatever means he could to stall his foster brother's case. A court date was finally set for the fall of 1937. When Alfred's attorney, Vincent Hallinan, and a United States Marshal arrived at Woodside to serve Whittell with a subpoena, an insult-spewing assistant met them at the padlocked gates. She threatened to use a loaded shotgun if they tried to enter the premises. The surreal confrontation took place while Whittell's agitated German shepherd threw itself against the gates and lions roared in the background. It took four days and numerous attempts before a determined court clerk, resorting to trickery, successfully served the subpoena.[5]

Despite the Barnum & Bailey atmosphere surrounding the case, the trial opened on September 24, 1937. Attorney Hallinan attempted to prove that Alfred was, in fact, the illegitimate child of George Whittell, Sr., and his secretary. Hallinan also went to great lengths to demonstrate that Junior had squandered the opportunities afforded him while Alfred had done nothing less than rise to the station he deserved.[6] "Every stepping stone upon which a man can set his foot on the path downward," asserted Hallinan, "George Whittell has tried." During his testimony, Alfred even accused Junior of experimenting with morphine. George, he asserted, always maintained that with judicious use, no harm was incurred.[7]

After seven years of battles, George and Alfred reached an undisclosed, out-of-court settlement. In the end, it appears that Alfred won little for his efforts. When the judge slammed his gavel down to seal the case, George was quoted as saying, "Well, that was short and sweet."[8]

Increasingly, Whittell retreated to Woodside, a comfortable home that had become his fortress. George, Sr., built the brick mansion in 1912 in the Renaissance Revival style with simple dignified columns and Romanesque arches. The estate was over 7,000 square feet, and with money, space, and servants, virtually every need was easily accommodated there. If it were not for Whittell's growing interest in Nevada, his leaving Woodside would have become increasingly rare.

Junior was pursuing many youthful distractions during the construction of Woodside, but when he inherited the property, he made modifications that reflected his tastes. Whittell added a hydraulic lift that delivered a full-sized movie projector into the dining room. With the push of a button, a screen descended from a niche above the living room fireplace, turning the home into a theater. Whittell liked the idea, but it wasn't enough. He constructed a separate theater outfitted with nothing but the best equipment. Tunnels connected buildings for easy, secret, weather-protected access.

The Whittell family home in Woodside was a large estate where an imaginative person with unlimited resources could indulge every whim. (Courtesy of Cecile Keefe)

Whittell retained his interest in wild animals, and his Woodside property had what a real estate flyer would later call an "elaborate, caged lions' run...set among the trees not far from the house." The sales brochure goes on to point out that "an additional lion cage is immediately outside the northwest solarium of the residence." (One cannot have too many lion runs!) With unlimited funds at his disposal, Whittell modified Woodside to suit his every whim, but his greatest building project, indeed his most important legacy, was still ahead of him.[9]

In 1936, at the age of fifty-four, Whittell took on the only project that he could truly claim as his own. Attracted by the Nevada tax structure, he began moving much of his business and his official residence to Reno in 1929.[10] An odd twist of fate shifted the millionaire's focus to the Tahoe Basin. Norman Biltz, a Nevada entrepreneur and real estate agent, related in an oral history how he and Whittell became involved in the acquisition of land at the Lake. Biltz and a partner from the Bay Area, Henry Trevor, had the opportunity to acquire twenty-seven miles of lakefront property on the Nevada side. This included roughly 100,000 acres of land that was

Whittell was fascinated with motion pictures. He obtained the state-of-the-art in professional film cameras and projectors. Above, Elia inspects his latest toy.

The land deal among partners Biltz, Trevor and George Whittell, left Whittell in possession of the eastern shore of Lake Tahoe from the northern state line to south of Cave Rock. The star on the above map marks the approximate location of the future Thunderbird Lodge. (Map from Lake of the Sky, Nevada Publications)

part of the Hobart estate, the holdings of the Carson & Tahoe Lumber & Fluming Company, and the Mills estate. Together the properties represented most of the Nevada side of the Tahoe Basin.[11]

Biltz and Trevor attracted the interest of a wealthy third partner from New York named Walter Seligman, who gave them the go-ahead to purchase the property. The arrangement called for two dollars for each foot of shore running two hundred feet deep and one dollar for each acre of hinterland. Biltz and Trevor put up between sixty and seventy thousand dollars to secure the land, with the balance, "roughly two million…due in some sixty or ninety days."[12] Seligman then backed out of the deal, leaving Biltz and Trevor with their investment in jeopardy. Biltz turned to his friend, George Whittell, for help.

According to Biltz, Whittell told him, "Norm, I don't like partners; I don't want to get involved. But I tell you what I'll do; I'll put up the money [and] I'll give you back your sixty, seventy thousand. …Then you go ahead and subdivide it and sell it, and when I get my money back (plus three percent interest) then you'll participate for twenty-five percent of the profits." Biltz recognized this immediately as a generous offer since their investment was restored, and they still had a chance

Norman Biltz, a real estate agent, was always on the lookout for a good deal. He was the author of the "One Sound State" campaign designed to attract the wealthy to Nevada's tax haven. Biltz persuaded his friend George Whittell to invest in Tahoe property. (from Nevadans and Nevada, 1950, by Boyd Moore, courtesy of the James Collection)

to profit. Whittell, however, placed two additional conditions on the deal: "One is that I don't want my estate involved in any joint ventures or partnerships. So you'll have to gamble that I'll live until you pay me back. …The other is so you don't prostitute this property, you don't give it away to get me paid off. I want to have approval of any prices you sell at." The partners signed an agreement to that effect.[13]

Biltz and Trevor immediately started looking for clients, hoping to earn Whittell's minimum and begin making money. Within two months, the two had secured enough commitments from people willing to purchase about 600,000 feet at prices ranging from seventy to eighty dollars a foot. When Whittell heard about the deals, he told Biltz that they were moving too fast and he was not going to approve any sales no matter how high the price. Since the millionaire had veto rights on all purchases, it was clear the two salesmen had been wasting their time. 🌿

Biltz and Trevor were so angry, they eventually went to Whittell with the agreement, and according to Biltz, "tore it up and threw it in his face, and spit in his face." In retrospect, Biltz realized it was a bad move. Whittell eventually did sell some of the land, and the two developers would have received a slight profit. Nonetheless, Biltz could only conclude, "I do believe, because of the sadistic nature of this individual, that if we had kept [the agreement]...he would not have sold any. He is a very hard man. This gave him great personal pleasure, to knock us out of the pot."[14] 🌿

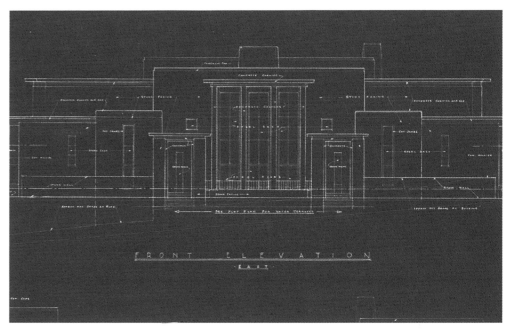

Whittell commissioned designs for two Tahoe-based casinos. He shelved both plans, but his concept for a Sand Harbor development would have produced an exclusive, fashionable playground for the rich and famous.

The pride of Whittell's series of flying machines was this DC2, which he named Thunderbird. *The Captain had this predecessor to the ubiquitous DC3 outfitted with a comfortable lounge.*

Whittell was now in control of nearly one-third of the Tahoe Basin including twenty-seven miles of Nevada shoreline. The possibilities excited local residents. The millionaire made it clear that he planned massive developments. His designs for a Sand Harbor Hotel and Casino, dated August 1938, demonstrate Whittell's capacity for looking to the future. It shows a project similar in size to casinos later constructed on the north and south shores of the Lake.[15] 🌿

Whittell also invested a great deal of time and money into aeronautics during this period. As a pilot and a connoisseur of technology, the Captain purchased the fastest transports he could find. Beginning in 1936, he experimented with the design of three large airplanes. His private air force included a Douglas DC-2, delivered on August 11, 1936, a date so early that the craft was a competitor for the first privately-owned luxury airline. Whittell staffed the plane with two pilots and a hostess. Fascinated with Native American motifs, he named the DC-2 "Thunderbird," a reference to a mythic creature that caused the heavens to roar.[16] 🌿

The Captain's Grumman G-21 "Goose" acquired a dubious reputation.

Nevada-native Frederick J. DeLongchamps (1882-1969) shaped Nevada and parts of California with designs for ten courthouses, and hundreds of commercial buildings, post offices, and homes. The Thunderbird Lodge survives as one of his most monumental legacies. (from Nevadans and Nevada, 1950, by Boyd Moore, courtesy of the James Collection)

A year later, he contracted with the Boeing Aircraft Company to deliver a customized Model 307 Stratoliner. Whittell's designs show an elaborate interior including sleeping suites for seven and a shower. A range of 3,300 miles would allow for a commute from California to France. In spite of the plans, however, Whittell never took delivery of the plane, perhaps because Elia did not enjoy flying and preferred other means to reach her European home.[17]

As he acquired land in the Lake Tahoe Basin, Whittell turned his attention to sea planes. In 1938, he purchased a Grumman G-21 "Goose." The plane crashed in September of that year during its first attempt at a landing into Lake Tahoe. The Captain had the wreckage raised, disassembled and reconditioned. Whittell sold the craft in 1939 after a second crash landing at the Lake. That same year he found a buyer for his seldom-used DC-2. Whittell would spend the rest of his life concentrating on terrestrial ways to indulge himself.[18]

Principal among these was Whittell's plans for the development of his Lake Tahoe holdings. This included the construction of a remarkable summer retreat. Soon after purchasing his Tahoe property, he began collaborating with noted Nevada architect Frederick DeLongchamps on the design of an isolated complex of buildings to serve as his summer home.

Throughout his six decades of practice, DeLongchamps worked hard to give his customers what they wanted. He folded himself around their needs, planning buildings that would be most appealing. By the 1930s, DeLongchamps was highly regarded with thirty years' experience. Dozens of his first designs went into production without major modification.[19] In the case of Whittell, however, the discussion was prolonged. The architect found in the capricious millionaire a client who rejected proposals and tinkered with details. Clearly, this would be a different sort of project.

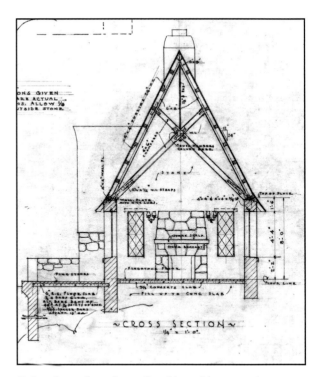

DeLongchamps designed a small card house, like most of the structures in the complex, to match the main lodge. (Courtesy of the Special Collections Department, University of Nevada, Reno Library)

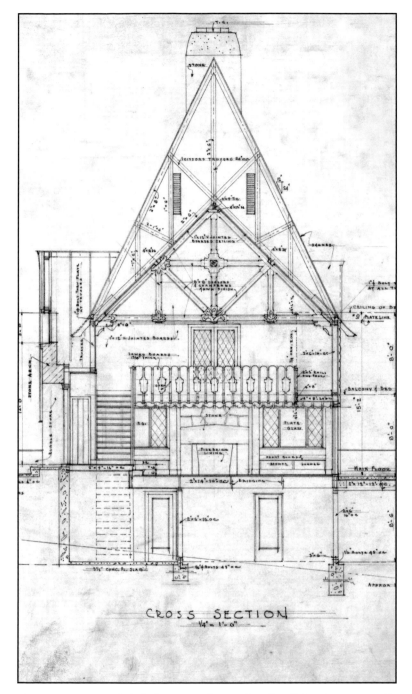

CROSS SECTION
¼" = 1'-0"

After experimenting with the look of a sprawling wooden cabin, DeLongchamps eventually designed a steep-roofed structure with a scissor-truss, shown in this early cross section dating to late 1936.

Of the more than 500 drawings that are part of the DeLongchamps Manuscripts in the Special Collections Department at the University of Nevada, Reno Library, the Whittell material illustrates one of the architect's most complicated, and perhaps frustrating, projects. DeLongchamps's original vision called for a squat, one-story mountain cabin finished with rustic appointments. The main floor included a living room, a kitchen, and three bedrooms. A small basement would have provided two servants' bedrooms, a bathroom, and a combination boiler/laundry room. The roof was moderately steep to accommodate snow loads, but it was hipped—its gables were clipped—giving the structure a low, horizontal feel. DeLongchamps finished these plans on June 12, 1936.[20]

Whittell quickly rejected almost every aspect of the proposal. The architect began work on a new design, and on August 4, 1936, he laid out an approach that included a steeper roof. This gave the structure the vertical proportions employed in the finished lodge. The log siding remained in this revised plan, with "random rubble stone" used for the chimney. By October 1936, Whittell

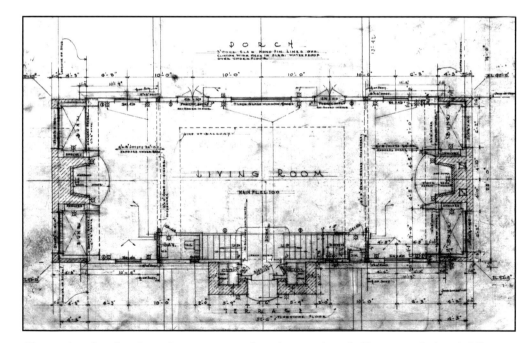

The first floor plan allowed for a large open space with fireplaces at either end. (Courtesy of the Special Collections Department, University of Nevada, Reno Library)

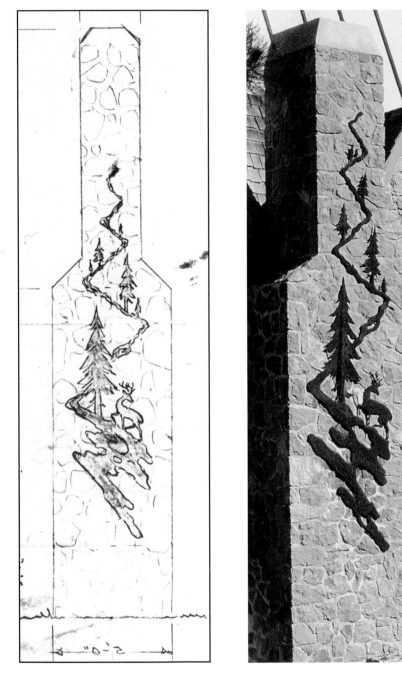

had accepted DeLongchamps's ideas for the interior of the main lodge. It took another year and numerous revisions before the Captain agreed with the architect's designs for the garage and several outbuildings.

The earliest mention of a stone treatment of the exterior dates to December 15, 1937. Plans for the garage read "stone to match main house," indicating that by the end of that year, Whittell had rejected a log cabin in favor of a random stone exterior. Many details, however, remained in flux. Even these drawings depict the garage with a steep roof to match the main lodge. The document gives no indication of the design that Whittell finally accepted, which called for a flat-roofed garage with a large lighthouse annex. Several approaches to the tunnel and the original boathouse date to early 1938, with revisions completed on April 7. Finally, construction could begin.

Random stones and delicate ironwork combine to give the Thunderbird Lodge its distinctive look. Here we see the DeLongchamps plan next to the finished stone and ironwork. (Drawing above left courtesy of Special Collections Department, University of Nevada, Reno Library; photograph above right, courtesy of Scott Klette).

Apprentice stonemasons from the Stewart Indian School south of Carson City constructed much of the Stewart campus, including this building. Graduates went on to build Whittell's estate at Tahoe. (Courtesy of the Nevada State Historic Preservation Office)

To give his mansion a unique look, Whittell employed Native American stone-masons trained at Carson City's Stewart Indian School in Nevada. The federal government founded the facility in 1890 to acculturate Northern Paiute, Washoe, and Shoshone American Indians of the Great Basin. Eventually, students representing several other western tribes also attended the school. Stewart provided Native American boys with instruction and experience in masonry; training intended to produce careers after graduation. Students constructed many of the Stewart Indian School buildings, creating a campus that today forms a remarkable district listed in the National Register of Historic Places. Stewart stonework also survives throughout Northern Nevada as evidence of the graduates' subsequent accomplishments. The Thunderbird Lodge complex is the largest off-campus undertaking of the Stewart masons, and it stands as a monument to their skill and artistry.[21]

Geese in flight are ready to decorate Whittell's castle. Antonio Soletti, the master ironworker, kneels in front. His apprentices, Luigi Manzon (l) and John Wessa (r), are standing. (Courtesy of the Soletti and Manzon families)

Descendants of the ironworkers have made available an extensive collection of approximately one hundred original drawings done for the finish work at the mansion. The drawings reveal an imaginative array of abstract designs and animals. (Courtesy of the Soletti and Manzon families)

To give his Tahoe castle added distinction, Whittell sought the services of Antonio Soletti and his Bay Area Italian ironworkers. Soletti was born in 1906 in the Alpine foothills northwest of Venice, Italy. Although his parents immigrated to California when he was a child, he remained behind with his grandparents because he had polio. As an apprentice, Soletti learned and perfected the art of decorative ironwork. By the time he arrived on the West Coast in the mid-1930s, the twenty-nine-year-old was already a skilled blacksmith. The craftsman then collaborated with other artists who were forming the Allied Arts Guild in Menlo Park, California.

While working for Whittell, Soletti established his own business called the San Mateo Iron and Artwork Company. He and his ironworkers forged elaborate details for Whittell's Tahoe estate, adorning large stone chimneys with fanciful woodland scenes. They crafted grates, lamps, fireplace screens, and countless other whimsical details that employ animal motifs, but most were not able to see their finished work in place. Because of the idiosyncratic wishes of the Captain, only Soletti himself was allowed on the grounds to install this remarkable assemblage of art.[22]

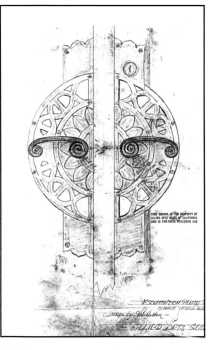

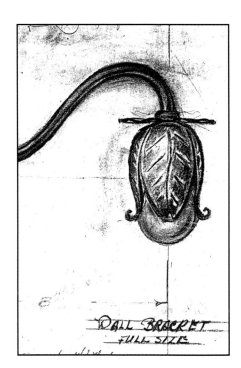

The many drawings completed before forging the iron details at the Whittell mansion included the thunderbird, locks and fittings for doors, lamps, fire screens, and (opposite) andirons. (Drawings courtesy of the Soletti and Manzon families; photograph upper right, courtesy of Scott Klette)

Completing the ethnic diversity of the project, Whittell hired Norwegian woodworkers. These carpenters gave balconies and ceilings a Scandinavian look. Exposed rafters in the Card House, for example, are distinctive for their patterned shaved edges.[23]

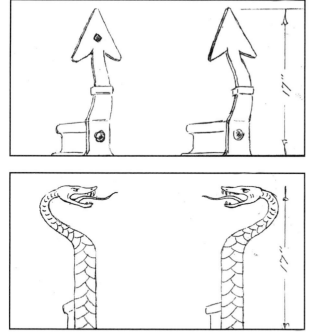

From door windows to brackets, the ironwork of Soletti gave graceful details to the buildings and grounds of Whittell's estate. (Photograph at top courtesy of Scott Klette)

The filed edges of roof beams give the carpentry of the various buildings a Scandinavian appearance. The Norwegian carpenters who completed the estate's woodwork built the Card House, shown above, without a false ceiling, exposing the building's steep roof. (Courtesy of Scott Klette)

The DeLongchamps plan called for a rich synthesis of design, masonry, ironwork, and carpentry. The estate also showcased carefully considered landscaping that exploited the property's steep descent to the Lake. The grounds featured an intricate system of waterfalls, streams, and pools flowing down and around the main lodge. Two of the lakeside pools have been filled in and are now covered with lawn, but clearly Whittell intended to surround the castle with a moat-like meandering band of running water, taking full advantage of the natural hillside and the magnificent views of the area.

This Page & Opposite Page: Whittell insisted that flowing water envelop the house. A carefully constructed course tumbled water down the hillside, then led it along channels to feed pools that once surrounded the main mansion. (Photograph opposite page, courtesy of Scott Klette)

Complementing the waterways, workers built footpaths and a variety of stone features all around the estate. An oft-repeated story maintains that frequently, when Whittell finished a late night of drinking and playing cards, he placed a whiskey bottle on the grounds to direct the next day's workers to lay paths and streams up to that point. Then, he retired to sleep off the effects of his excesses.[24]

This Page & Opposite Page: The stonework decorating the grounds of the Thunderbird Lodge includes whimsical hogan-like structures, meandering paths, a dragon bridge, and a lighthouse. The winding trail shown on the opposite page, right, represents the tail of a giant dragon. (Courtesy of Scott Klette; photograph at bottom right, courtesy of Vance Fox)

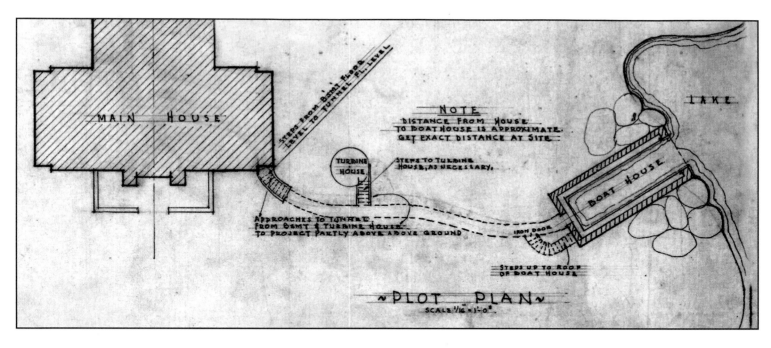

PLOT PLAN
SCALE 1/16"=1'-0".

MAIN HOUSE

NOTE
DISTANCE FROM HOUSE TO BOATHOUSE IS APPROXIMATE. GET EXACT DISTANCE AT SITE.

TURBINE HOUSE

STEPS TO TURBINE HOUSE, AS NECESSARY.

STEPS FROM BSMT FLOOR LEVEL TO TUNNEL FL. LEVEL

APPROACHES TO TUNNEL FROM BSMT & TURBINE HOUSE TO PROJECT PARTLY ABOVE ABOVE GROUND

IRON DOOR

STEPS UP TO ROOF OF BOAT HOUSE

BOAT HOUSE

LAKE

Left: DeLongchamps originally designed a short tunnel between the main lodge and the original boat-house. It also provided underground access to a small structure that housed an electricity-generating turbine. In late 1939, workers extended the tunnel several hundred feet. (Courtesy of the Special Collections Department, University of Nevada, Reno Library)

Below & Opposite Page: A dungeon-like tunnel extending over 500 feet connects several buildings on the Thunderbird Lodge grounds. The Card House entrance to the tunnel was through a bathroom shower. (Courtesy of Scott Klette)

One of the more amazing elements of the Thunderbird grounds is the nearly 600 feet of tunnel that connect the main lodge with the Card House, the original boathouse, and the new boathouse. Rocks scattered throughout the area show the remains of blast holes like those found near historic underground mines. Clearly much of the rock used in the landscaping came from the construction of the tunnel. One story surrounding the building of the Lodge maintains that Cornish miners from the famed Comstock Mining District blasted and excavated Whittell's subterranean passageway. They would have been an

obvious source of labor. DeLongchamps was heavily involved in Nevada's mining industry, and the Great Depression left scores of talented, experienced miners unemployed.[25]

At its deepest, the tunnel bores through granite almost three stories below ground. Meticulously sheathed with slate, the barrel-vaulted passage resembles a secret corridor below a medieval castle. Not even Europe's best, however, were likely to feature an African lion with full mane ambling along, in search of a cool spot to take a nap. According to Lodge visitors, the cold storage room was one of Bill's favorite retreats.

At first, the tunnel was only 70 feet long, connecting the basement of the main lodge to the original boathouse. An extension measuring 185 feet brought the underground passage some 18 feet below the Card House. A steel spiral staircase led up to a hidden door in the shower. The tunnel then proceeded nearly 110 feet to a lake access point where supplies could be loaded from a boat docked in deep water. A rail system allowed a cart to roll heavier burdens along the length of the tunnel.

Thunderbird (as she appeared before later alterations) awaits her Captain in a boathouse made specifically for the magnificent vessel.

Within months of the completion of the complex, the design of a new yacht named Thunderbird made the first boathouse obsolete. Whittell commissioned a second boathouse that would be over 100 feet in length and 27 feet wide. Its 90-foot channel accommodated Thunderbird and an additional craft, if necessary. Workers blasted a longer tunnel to the new location.

Whittell's latest development required a split in the tunnel once it reached over 300 feet from the Lodge, past the entrance to the Card House. The extension brought the total length of the main

Whittell had carpenters install a one-way mirror in the lodge's front door so that he or his staff could secretly peer at guests.

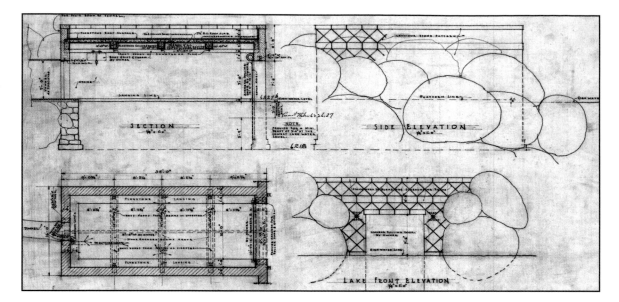

Above & Opposite: DeLongchamps designs depict various stages in the planning for the main lodge and the boathouse. The front façade for the lodge is nearly as built, but it lacks the prominent chimneys in the front. (Courtesy of the Special Collections Department, University of Nevada, Reno Library)

When the original boathouse was too small to serve the new Thunderbird speedboat, Whittell ordered the structure's conversion into an indoor swimming pool. During construction, a laborer fell and died. Whittell abandoned the project and left the tools in place, where they lie to this day. (Courtesy of Scott Klette)

passage to almost 500 feet. Together with the now useless extension to the lake, workers had excavated roughly 550 feet of tunnel, most of which was carved through solid granite.

The Captain subsequently considered additional alterations to his lakeside castle. He decided to convert the old boathouse into an indoor pool by walling off the entrance with glass block. He then had the sides finished with concrete, but tradition maintains tragedy struck when a workman fell from his ladder and broke his neck. Whittell immediately stopped the project. He abandoned the ladder and other equipment where they lay and closed off the room.[26]

There were also other ideas for changes. Plans dated September 17, 1940, would have dramatically rearranged and expanded the main floor of the mansion. Whittell did not implement these or DeLongchamps's 1955 redesign of the garage wing into a combination of living quarters, kitchen, and large dining room. In spite of the proposed alterations, the Captain ultimately kept the estate much as it was originally built.[27]

Gadgets found today at the Thunderbird Lodge make it clear that Whittell's fascination with modern technology did not pass with his youth. The main door to the mansion includes a one-way glass portal that allowed the reclusive millionaire to peer

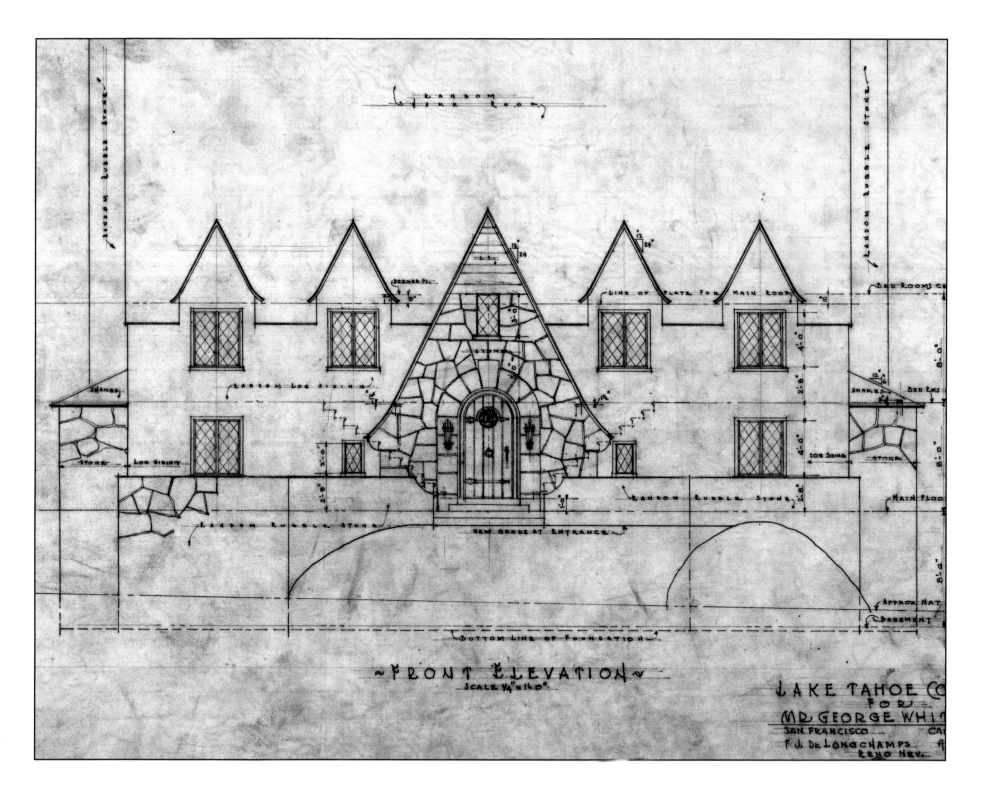

~FRONT ELEVATION~

SCALE 1/4"=1'0"

LAKE TAHOE CO
FOR
MR. GEORGE WHI
SAN FRANCISCO   CAL
F. J. DE LONGCHAMPS   A
RENO NEV.

Above Left: A control panel stands ready to connect and operate gadgets in the lodge's great room. Above Right: The Captain and his guests viewed Hollywood's latest with the help of a projector from the Strong Electric Corporation of Toledo, Ohio. Bottom Left & Right: Whittell purchased state-of-the-art gauges for use at the Thunderbird Lodge. (All photographs except bottom right courtesy of Ron James)

secretly at arriving guests. Whittell installed a security system that warned of intruders, a state-of-the-art barometer to keep track of the weather, and a range-finding siting scope for surveying his vast estate. An intricate control panel made it possible to lower a hidden movie screen and to operate a projector, much like mechanisms he had installed at his California home. In the '40s, Whittell also constructed a television antenna at Lake Tahoe similar to the one at Woodside. An August 1949 television guide from the American Broadcasting Corporation, found among Whittell's effects at the Thunderbird Lodge, indicates that he employed this new piece of technology early in the industry's history.[28]

Papers left at the Lodge also include instructions for a "Photo-electric Pilot: Automatic Steering Device for Pleasure and Commercial Craft" and for a 1937 "Photo Electric Relay," a light-sensitive electrical switch.[29] A wall in Whittell's bedroom features an instrument panel with an indoor/outdoor temperature gauge, indicators for wind velocity and direction, and a barometer. Inside the boathouse is a "liquidometer," a relic that once gauged the fuel levels in reserve tanks for the boat.

Large radio speakers that were apparently obtained as war surplus blared music that could be heard for miles around the Lake. At the same time, hidden miniature microphones helped the Captain eavesdrop on the conversations of guests and servants. Sensors allowed him to gauge the arrival of visitors and those who dared to trespass. Clearly, a sly, secretive Whittell was enamored with the technologically inventive twentieth century.[30]

Whittell had owned many speedboats, always seeking the best. In 1939, he summoned John L. Hacker, renowned wooden boat designer, to Woodside to discuss a project that would set a higher standard of excellence for the wooden boat industry. The result was one of the Captains most valued prizes, *Thunderbird*, a yacht filled with the latest technology. That alone, however, did not make her one of the great wooden vessels of the century. The famed naval designer had an impeccable reputation, and he answered the challenge with a sleek, Honduras mahogany craft featuring stainless steel trim. During a test run, the fully loaded yacht clocked 43.1 miles per hour.[31] This work of art could cut through the waves as fast as any boat at the Lake and with a style unmatched. It was the Captain's Duesenberg of the water.

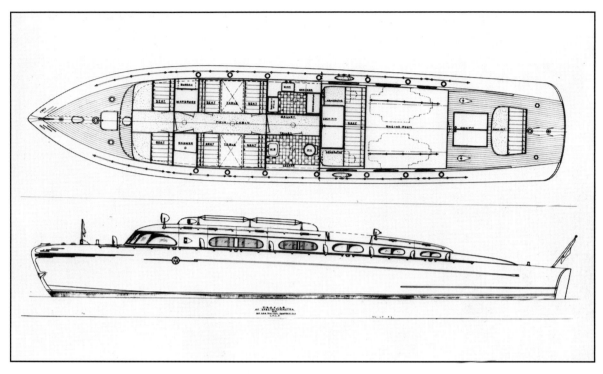

Famed marine architect John Hacker drafted plans for the yacht, Thunderbird, in 1939.

Huskin Boat and Motor Works in Bay City, Michigan, built Thunderbird, shown here in transit.

Casino mogul William Fisk Harrah purchased the Thunderbird, subsequently replacing the engines and adding a flying bridge.

According to Hackercraft historian James P. Barry, Whittell's fifty-five-foot speedboat with its twelve-foot beam was "Hacker's ultimate commuter." Barry also notes that Whittell's commission recalled the millionaire's fascination with flight. Thunderbird's "profile was streamlined like that of an aircraft. The cabin was long and low, the forward end of it a control station separated from the cabin proper by a partition with a door, rather like the pilot's space on a commercial passenger aircraft." The cabin included mahogany paneling, red leather upholstery, electric heat with window defrosters, and faucets with hot water. A phone system allowed for communication throughout the vessel and ship-to-shore. Whittell's new toy was so remarkable, the journal Yachting published an article on it illustrated with plans in 1941.[32] ✒

Thunderbird first crossed the mountain lake's blue waters on July 14, 1940.[33] She originally sported twin Kermath 550-hp engines that gave her the power to outrace all challengers. Despite her

The low-flying Thunderbird *clocked speeds of over 40 m.p.h. during her first test run. Whittell insisted that the boat be outfitted with the latest technology and all the comforts of home.*

potential, *Thunderbird* remained hidden within the Lodge's boathouse, becoming a legend that appeared phantom-like only when Whittell visited the Lake during the summer, and then only when it fancied him to take her for a spin. Part of the voluminous folklore about the Captain includes the assertion that he purposefully kept his beloved speedboat hidden during World War II, afraid that the U. S. government might conscript her into military service. Whether or not that was the motive, the story offered Lake residents an explanation for the rarity of *Thunderbird* sightings. ✒

Thunderbird, shortly after construction, tests the water in Michigan.

Opposite Page: The stunningly beautiful Thunderbird *occasionally visits the boathouse that was once her home. (Photograph courtesy of Scott Klette)*

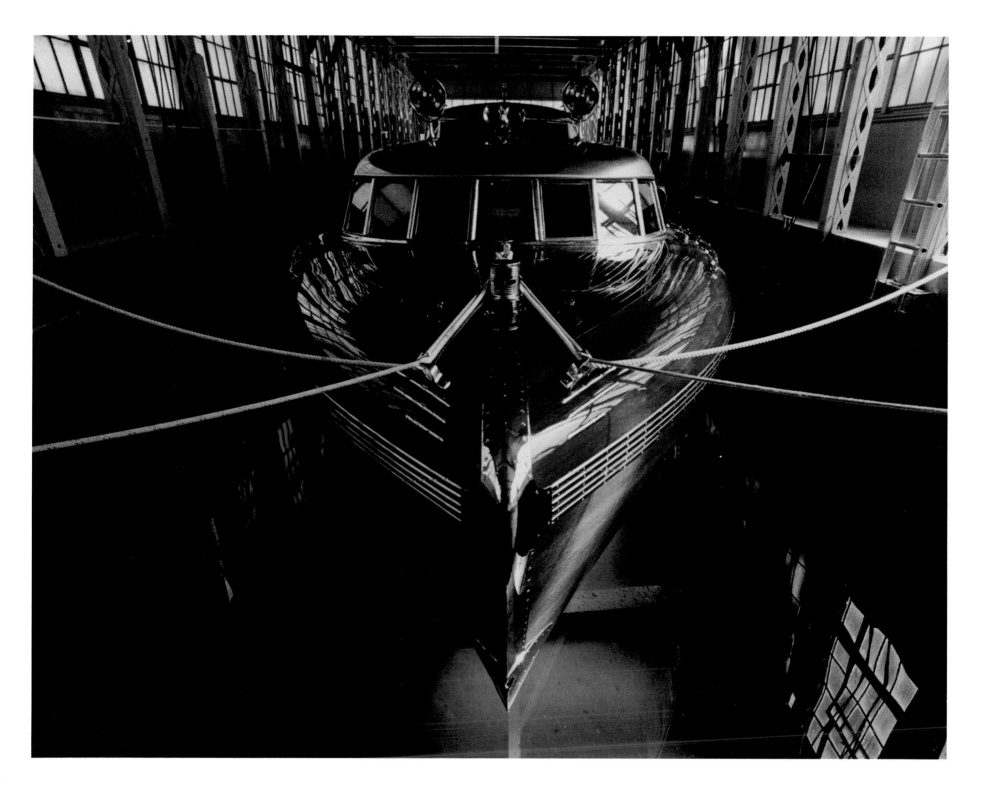

Above & Opposite Page: The Card House was the site of many poker games. Legend would later claim that hundreds of thousands of dollars changed hands with the luck of the draw. (Photograph opposite, courtesy of Vance Fox)

Understanding Whittell's life at Lake Tahoe requires a glimpse through two separate lenses. Whittell allegedly hosted wild parties for actors, politicians, former presidents, and another notoriously reclusive millionaire, Howard Hughes. Stories that feature the Captain riding a horse across the grounds while chasing naked guests cannot be substantiated. They almost certainly are fabrications spawned by neighbors who could only speculate about the social life of Lake Tahoe's wealthy mystery man. The claim that Whittell once entertained visitors with three trumpeting elephants standing atop their private barn cannot be true since he tried only once, unsuccessfully, to bring a single pachyderm to Tahoe. Paul Laxalt, who served as Whittell's attorney in the 1950s before becoming Nevada's governor, recalled hearing of the tycoon's wild parties. Laxalt said there was even a story of a reveler who died, remaining seated in a chair for several hours before anyone noticed.[34]

Contrary to later folklore, the aging millionaire became increasingly private, replacing a fast-paced, hard-hitting life with less conspicuous self-indulgence. The reality during the 1930s and '40s was that next to no information, wild or otherwise, could be gathered from Tahoe's quiet east shore.

As a local newspaper, the Tahoe Tattler, reported in 1939, it is "as hard to confirm news about a European Government [as it is about]

Lake Tahoe's land-owning George Whittell." Tahoe residents were starved for details about the life of the wealthy addition to their midst, but this tycoon was elusive, rarely offering glimpses into his activities. The lack of information inspired excitement and interest. The Tattler asserted, "Multimillionaires are always news. When they are retired, eccentric, publicity-shy, they are more news."[35] Generally, tales that leaked out were incomplete or later proven wrong. ❧

A few things are clear. Whittell had a profound interest in poker and alcohol, and he had a small number of associates with whom he was willing to share his time. An elderly Ty Cobb, once a star of the baseball diamond, played cards with him, as did a few other men, hand-picked for their willingness to gamble thousands and drink heavily. Veiled in secrecy, these games moved from place to place along the lakeshore as a deterrent to thieves who might strike while fortunes were being won and lost. A hidden safe at the Thunderbird Lodge hints at Whittell's concern for security, no doubt heightened by his preference for wagering tens of thousands of dollars in cash. ❧

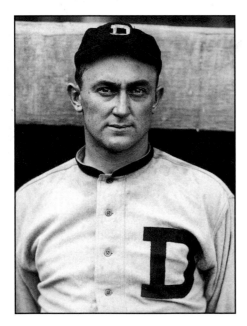

Famed baseball star Tyrus Raymond "Ty" Cobb (1886-1961) as a young man. He retired to Lake Tahoe where he became the Captain's gambling companion. (Courtesy of Corbis Images)

Whittell also never lost his penchant for beautiful women, and stories persist about the casino showgirls he sneaked into his private poker games. There was, however, a serious obstacle to this sort of indulgence. The aging playboy took a chance when he brought the young dancers to the Card House by way of the tunnel. According to Donald Mason, who served as butler at the mansion for two summers as a young man, Whittell was not concerned about the reaction of his wife Elia, who typically spent the season in France before the outbreak of World War II.

The Card House interior today. (Courtesy of Vance Fox)

Instead, Mason said that the Captain was worried about Mae Mollhagen, his housekeeper and principal mistress.[36]

The former butler went on to recall that the situation was often more complicated than an attempt to hide an indiscretion. Mason, who later became a priest, also recalled that when Mae and the Captain fought, Whittell often recruited the young butler for an evening of gambling at the North Shore's Cal-Neva Casino. They frequently returned home with showgirls, whom Whittell entertained in the main hall of the Lodge, the whole time watching Mae's bedroom door, hoping that he would make her jealous.

Whittell continued his life at Lake Tahoe as an enigmatic, self-indulgent millionaire, but as always, he was capable of demonstrating another side of his character. May 17, 1941, offered one of those rare occasions when the Captain emerged from the shadows in a more positive light. That afternoon, the packet steamer *Marian B*, with its crew of three, was lost in Tahoe's rough waters. The boat had left Glenbrook and was on its way to Brockway, but it never arrived at its destination. Whittell was the first to organize a rescue party, sending out his *Thunderbird* with searchlights into the night. Two bodies were found a few days later. The *Marian B* had burned and all hands were lost.[37] Having done his good deed, Whittell retreated again into the privacy of his estate.

Mae Mollhagen and her brother Jimmy in a restaurant photo capturing the two in San Francisco in 1941.

Chapter 2 Notes

[1] "Last Will and Testament of Anna Whittell and George Whittell." TLPS Archive.

[2] "Woman Sues George Whittell for Whipping at 'Party.'" *San Francisco Chronicle* (May 17, 1930).

[3] "Jury Chosen to Hear Suit for $25,000." *San Francisco Chronicle* (March 10, 1933); "Girl Whipping Case Goes to Jurors Today." *San Francisco Chronicle* (March 15, 1933); "'Whipping' Party Victim Awarded $5,062 by Jury." *San Francisco Chronicle* (March 16, 1933).

[4] "Merry Capt. Whittell's Pet Lion Plays a $200,000 Joke." *American Weekly*, 1934.

[5] "Affidavit for Order Requiring Presence of Party: Alfred vs. George Whittell, Jr., et. al." TLPS Archive; "No Process Serving when a Lion's about." *San Francisco Chronicle* (December 19, 1958). See TLPS Archive for 1930s newspaper clippings of unclear provenience.

[6] "Whittell Will Case Bares Family Drama." *San Francisco Chronicle* (September 24, 1937).

[7] "Capt. Whittell Accused of Taking Dope." *San Francisco Chronicle* (September 25, 1937).

[8] "Whittell Estate Battle Settled out of Court." *San Francisco Chronicle* (January 7, 1938). "Whittells Meet in Court." *San Francisco Chronicle* (September 28, 1937); See also newspaper clipping without provenience dated September 2, 1937, TLPS Archive; "Whittell Brothers." *San Mateo County Times* (October 23, 1998).

[9] TLPS Archive preserves material on the Woodside estate, including modifications made by the Captain.

[10] "Articles of Incorporation of George Whittell and Company, Inc." (Nevada State Archives, Nevada State Library and Archives, Department of Cultural Affairs: 1929). See also other documents in the Nevada State Archives associated with the development of Whittell's business in Nevada.

[11] Douglas H. Strong, *Tahoe: An Environmental History* (Lincoln: University of Nebraska Press, 1984), provides a good overview of the land transactions that occurred on the east side of the Tahoe Basin.

[12] Norman H. Biltz, *Memoirs of "Duke of Nevada": Developments of Lake Tahoe, California and Nevada, Reminiscences of Nevada Political and Financial Life.* (Reno, Nevada: University of Nevada, Reno, Oral History Program, 1969); "Whittell Buys 18,000 Acres on Lake Tahoe." *San Francisco Chronicle* (December 3, 1937); "Whittell Buys 10,000 More Acres at Tahoe." *San Francisco Chronicle* (December 18, 1937); "Whittell Buys New Property." *Tahoe Tattler* (December 17, 1937).

[13] Biltz, *Memoirs of "Duke of Nevada."*

[14] *Ibid.*

[15] Plans for the casino are preserved in the TLPS Archive. *San Francisco Chronicle* (December 18, 1937); "All-Year Resort to be Built at Incline." *Tahoe Tattler* (July 8, 1938); "Building to Start on Whittell Hotel Shortly, Report." *Tahoe Tattler* (July 15, 1938); "Construction to Begin on Whittell Casino August 20." *Tahoe Tattler* (July 29, 1938); "Whittell Awaits Snow Sports before Building." *Tahoe Tattler* (August 19, 1938); "Million Dollar Building Program at Tahoe," *Record Courier* (Douglas County, Nevada; December 24, 1937).

[16] John C. Ross, "The Short Life of George Whittell's Air Force." (Prepared for the Thunderbird Lodge Preservation Society, November 2002, revised June 2003), TLPS Archive; "George Whittell to Abandon Planes, Buy Yacht, Report." *Tahoe Tattler* (July 21, 1939); "Whittell Buys Huge Luxury Air Yacht." *San Francisco Chronicle* (March 13, 1937); "Whittell Plans Radio Station to Aid Flying." *Tahoe Tattler* (June 21, 1940); "Around the Lake." *Tahoe Tattler* (August 12, 1938).

[17] Plans for Whittell's 307 Stratoliner are preserved at the TLPS Archive. See also Ross, "The Short Life of George Whittell's Air Force."

[18] Ross, "The Short Life of George Whittell's Air Force."

[19] Ronald M. James, "Nevada's Historic Architect," *Nevada: The Magazine of the Real West* (August 1994), reprinted in *The Historical Nevada Magazine: Outstanding Historical Features from the Pages of Nevada Magazine* (Carson City: Nevada Magazine, 1998).

[20] See the "Whittell Lodge" file in the DeLongchamps Collection at the Special Collections Department, University of Nevada, Reno Library.

[21] Kent L. Seavey, "Stewart Indian School." Nomination for listing in the National Register of Historic Places (1985) on file at the Nevada State Historic Preservation Office, Department of Cultural Affairs, Carson City, Nevada.

[22] Information about Antonio Soletti and his ironworkers comes largely from Larry Soletti, his son, who has given presentations at the Lodge and has been available on many occasions to answer questions about his father's involvement. In addition, he and his family donated a large collection of original drawings to the TLPS Archive. The ironworkers used the drawings to fashion their ornamentations.

[23] Information about the Norwegian carpenters comes mainly from former TLPS director Phil Caterino who was able to interview some of the workers.

[24] People involved in the construction related many stories like these to Caterino.

[25] For DeLongchamps and mining see James, "Nevada's Historic Architect." For Cornish Miners and the Comstock see Ronald M. James, "Defining the Group: Nineteenth-Century Cornish on the Mining Frontier," Cornish Studies 2, ed. by Philip Payton (Exeter, UK: University of Exeter, 1994).

[26] Former TLPS director Phil Caterino heard this story from numerous people associated with the Lodge and its construction. Verification of the incident in records is problematic.

[27] "Whittell Lodge" file in the DeLongchamps Collection at the Special Collections Department, University of Nevada, Reno Library.

[28] TLPS Archive. See also Karen Barney and Bill Dohrmann, "Interview with Warren Crane, George Whittell's Personal Engineer." (October 17, 2002) TLPS Archive.

[29] TLPS Archive.

[30] Barney and Dohrmann, "Interview with Warren Crane."

[31] *Yachting*, March 1941 (67).

[32] James P. Barry, *Hackercraft*, (St. Paul, Minnesota: MBI Publishing, 2002), 95-98. Folklore suggests that the yacht was originally 56 feet long, and that due to damage to the stern of the boat, craftsmen later trimmed the vessel to 55 feet. Primary sources indicate it was always 55 feet. *Yachting*, March 1941 (67). See also memo from "Lloyd" to "Shep," September 3, 1962, regarding the sale of the boat and Whittell's assertion that it was 55 feet not 56 feet, TLPS Archive; "New Harbor under way as Captain Tries New Speedboat." *Tahoe Tattler* (July 28, 1939); "Biggest Tahoe Boat Launched for Whittell." *Tahoe Tattler* (July 19, 1940); "Second 1940 Win Gives Dollar Title." *Tahoe Tattler* (August 16, 1940); "Lou Fageol Wins Speed Boat Championship." *Tahoe Tattler* (July 25, 1941).

[33] "Biggest Tahoe Boat Launched For Whittell." *Tahoe Tattler* (July 19, 1940).

[34] Edward B. Scott, *The Saga of Lake Tahoe*. (Crystal Bay, Nevada: Sierra Tahoe Publishing, 1954) 311-312; "Flying Horses, Falling Planes Save the Captain from Ennui (You Know, Boredom)." *Tahoe Tattler* (September 12, 13, 1938); Paul Laxalt, *Nevada's Paul Laxalt: A Memoir*. (Reno, Nevada: Jack Bacon and Company, 2000) 74-78.

[35] "George Whittell to Abandon Planes, Buy Yacht, Report." *Tahoe Tattler* (July 21, 1939); "Whittell Unwittingly Makes Headlines." *Tahoe Tattler* (June 23, 1939).

[36] Fr. Don Mason, letter dated March 14, 1985, TLPS Archive; see also Barney and Dohrmann, "Interview with Warren Crane."

[37] "Tahoe Motor Launch Lost." *Nevada State Journal* (May 18, 1941).

Harsh winters at Lake Tahoe prevented the Captain from visiting his mountain retreat.

ONALD MASON RETURNED TO SERVE AGAIN AS BUTLER AT THE THUNDERBIRD LODGE IN 1942. HE FOUND A CHANGED PLACE AND A TRANSFORMED CAPTAIN, WRITING THAT "MEALS . . . WERE QUIETER, ALMOST SULLEN; AND ONLY RARELY DID WE GO TO THE CAL-NEVA; AND THEN HE WOULD GO WITH [MAE], WITH HER DRIVING INSTEAD OF ME. THIS TIME, TOO, HE DID NOT TAKE THE BOAT OUT ONCE; JUST SAT AND LOOKED AT THE LAKE MOST OF THE DAY." MORE IMPORTANTLY, MASON "RARELY FOUND SIGNS OF [MAE] HAVING STAYED IN HIS BEDROOM," AND "THE TWO OF THEM DRANK MUCH LESS."[1]

Mae, the Captain's beloved maid and mistress, died in an automobile crash in 1954. Whittell had the crumbled remains of the vehicle hauled to a hilltop overlooking the Lodge.

Opposite Page: Whittell built his Lodge in a remote location that kept people at a distance. Old age accentuated his reclusive nature.

With World War II, Whittell confronted the beginning of a new phase of his life when he could not participate in exciting world events. The crisis further insulted him when a lack of meat ration coupons forced him to surrender some of his pet carnivores to the San Francisco Zoo. A part of the young, flamboyant Whittell retired with them, but fortunately Bill remained with his beloved master.[2]

The life of a hedonist born to wealth often follows a familiar pattern. The exuberant excesses of youth eventually give way to a slower-paced consumption of pleasure. In one's later years, a lack of purpose and access to unlimited money can provide fertile soil for the enigmatic and eccentric to mutate into cloistered decadence.

The early 1950s saw increasing isolation and pain for the Captain. In 1953, his estranged foster brother, Alfred, died, failing to live through his sixties. Although the brothers had not been close, Whittell now had no one left who shared his earliest years. A year later, the Captain suffered yet another loss. Mae was driving home on Highway 28 around Lake Tahoe, returning from shopping at King's Beach, when she demolished her car and died. "He loved Mae deeply; I mean really loved her," former butler Donald Mason would later write. In that accident, Whittell lost one of his best friends.[3]

A Lake Tahoe story about the aftermath of Mae's death tells of the Captain playing morbid dirges. After weeks of this loud display of mourning, nearby

Due to a severe break in his leg, Whittell was limited, for the most part, to a wheelchair in his later years.

residents grew impatient with the intrusion, but since none of his neighbors really knew him, they were reluctant to ask the reclusive tycoon to stop the music. Warren Crane, Whittell's mechanic, maintains the incident never happened, and that the sound of the dirges was contained within the house. Once again, the Captain's ability to attract folklore surrounded him with stories of excess.[4]

In a more private expression of grief, Whittell had the remnants of Mae's woody station wagon towed to a prominent outlook above the Thunderbird Lodge. It rested there for forty-five years until 1999, when the U.S. Forest Service unwittingly hauled the revered cenotaph away as junk.

Also during this period, Whittell broke his leg twice, sustaining injuries that would change the rest of his life. The first time, Bill rolled over him and broke his lower leg. That injury healed reasonably well, but in the winter of 1955-56, he fell in the bathtub and shattered his upper leg. The break was severe enough to require screws, and it caused him a great deal of pain. Eventually, a portable x-ray machine brought to Woodside revealed that one of the screws had come loose. The Captain refused to address the problem with further surgery and instead used painkillers that caused him to lose interest in everything around him.

Whittell's interest in the Duesenberg is famous among automobile collectors. He ordered six and assisted in their design and final appointment. The 1930 Murphy Speedster, model number JO-120, is pictured here. He drove it less than a dozen times. (Courtesy of Automobile Quarterly)

The subject of Whittell's second broken leg became shrouded in the folklore that perpetually surrounded him. The aging adventurer probably preferred the story that one of his lions rolled over on him, or that he had been injured in a shooting accident. Certainly either one was more glamorous than slipping in the bathtub. Regardless of what really happened, recovery was limited. Now in his seventies, the Captain spent an increasing amount of time in a bathrobe and a wheelchair, making visits from Woodside to the rugged setting of Lake Tahoe a challenge.[5]

One of the few sources of joy for the elderly tycoon during the early 1950s was his growing friendship with a young man named John Lewis, Jr., the son of Whittell's California-based lawyer. Lewis was fascinated with Duesenbergs, and he wrote a letter to the elderly Captain, asking to see his collection. Whittell said yes and invited him to dinner. Before long, Lewis became the wealthy recluse's confidant and primary assistant, and for his twenty-first birthday in 1953, Whittell gave him one of his six Duesenbergs.[6] 🌿

A frequent guest at Whittell's estates, Lewis witnessed the millionaire's last years. He recalled the Captain with Elia, home from her summers in Paris, having dinner at Woodside, the couple speaking French so the servants couldn't eavesdrop. Elia had an apartment in San Francisco, but she returned to Woodside for weekends. The passion of a young marriage had vanished years before, replaced by a deep friendship and shared mutual respect. 🌿

In the late 1950s, Whittell secured the services of another young, ambitious man to serve as his Nevada-based attorney. Paul Laxalt was the son of a Basque sheepherder who had rented Sierra grazing rights from the Captain. Laxalt had been raised on stories of wild parties at "Whittell's Play Pen" with big cats among the guests. "Although I never could quite accept it," he would later write in his memoirs, "some witnesses even stated that a lion or tiger would occasionally stroll among the partygoers."[7] 🌿

The Thunderbird Lodge that Laxalt visited, however, did not rise to that reputation. The young lawyer recalls that Whittell's nurse Ruth Casey led him "into a huge gloomy room with fireplaces at both ends. On a porch adjoining the room were some thirty or forty myna birds, with whom the Captain conversed regularly." Laxalt was surprised to find the tycoon in a wheelchair, old and disabled, yet "he had a huge, distinguished, lion-sized head and piercing eyes" that could still twinkle. 🌿

Whittell had become increasingly private with age. While he attempted to retreat from the world, many people now came to him. The Captain was not, by nature, a generous man. Wealth and business were private matters, and he cared little about public accolades. He never used a donation to inspire the building of a monument to himself. On the other hand, Whittell was not completely opposed to requests for charitable contributions. He was old, and with no one to take on his financial empire, he was free to support good causes.[8] 🌿

In 1959, partly at the suggestion of Laxalt, the Captain donated large tracts of Little Valley near the Tahoe Basin to the University of Nevada, St. Mary's Hospital in Reno, and the Sisters of Charity in Carson City. In response, the University awarded Whittell an honorary

An elderly but still stylish Elia Whittell preparing for dinner in Woodside.

Perpetually drawn to animals, Whittell kept myna birds in his old age. Paul Laxalt, his Nevada-based attorney, recalled first meeting the millionaire surrounded by a flock of these birds.

doctorate in 1960, even though he neither sought nor wanted public praise. When approached by Nevada's Douglas County at the south end of the Lake, he responded with yet another donation of land, providing the real estate needed for a school. Named George Whittell High School, it was once again the sort of recognition the Captain shunned.[9]

In spite of these minor gifts of land, most of the Nevada side of Lake Tahoe remained undeveloped. Although Whittell made plans for lavish casinos and commercial development of his Tahoe property, he continued his life-long edict to do as little as possible to make money. The designs gathered dust, but by leaving the land untouched, Whittell's holdings increased in value. These pristine tracts of some of the most beautiful real estate in the world were now worth a fortune.

In yet another twist of fate, the persistence of Nevada's conservation efforts eventually offended Whittell so much that he pursued development. In 1958, shortly before the millionaire had donated land to the state university, Nevada's Governor Charles Russell persuaded the Captain to make roughly nine acres of Sand Harbor available to State Parks for a public beach. For years, people had sneaked across his property to enjoy the water. By granting access to a small part of his lakefront, Whittell hoped that the trespassing elsewhere would stop.

In the waning days of Nevada Governor Charles Russell's administration, Whittell made several donations of Lake property. He and the Republican governor had an affable relationship that brought out the Captain's generous side.

Unfortunately for the Captain, State Parks officials wanted more. In 1959, Grant Sawyer became Nevada's governor, and he began a relentless campaign to obtain additional acres for an immense Tahoe state park dedicated to the perpetual conservation of the environmentally sensitive land. Whittell's answer to Sawyer and State Parks was a firm no.

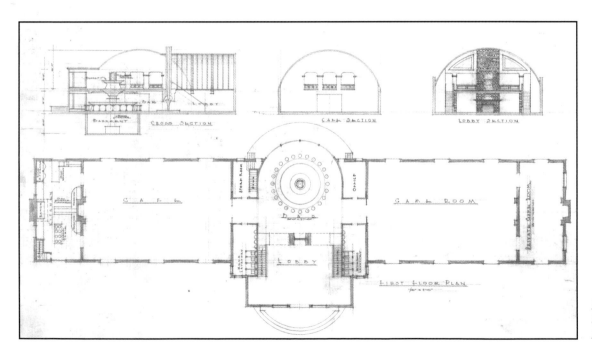

Plans for a casino at Zephyr Cove, which was to be built along the sandy beach north of the existing Zephyr Cove Lodge.

Nevada's chief executive decided that a face-to-face confrontation was in order. As Sawyer recalled in his oral history, "I flew [to the Bay Area] on a secret mission and went out to his house [in Woodside] and met his wife...but I didn't get any further than the kitchen, and she refused to let me speak to him, although I knew very well that he was in the house." When the Captain learned about the unwelcome visitor, he called the local sheriff and ordered his arrest. The sheriff came to the estate, but refused to file charges against the governor of Nevada. Instead, he escorted Sawyer off the property.[10]

The State of Nevada answered Whittell's recalcitrant attitude with a lawsuit, expecting judicial enforcement of a public condemnation of land. The Captain's response was swift. He cut off negotiations with the University of Nevada, which was hoping for a donation of more property. Whittell refused to do business with an entity that was taking him to court. The University claimed that it was not a state agency, an argument that failed immediately. There were no more gifts.

Whittell then sold 14.5 square miles of the northern part of his Tahoe estate to the Nevada Lake Tahoe Investment Company for $5,000,000 in 1959. The following year the property passed to the Crystal Bay Development Company for $25,000,000. It was clear that the Captain would rather see the land developed than lose it through judicial action. The Crystal Bay Company organized its holdings into what the developers hoped would be a $300,000,000 piece of real estate with thousands of new Basin residents. The newly created Incline Village clearly indicated how easily Whittell's open space could turn into congested communities filled with people attempting to retreat to the wilderness of the Tahoe Basin.[11]

Three decades of Whittell's ownership left much of Lake Tahoe's eastern shore undeveloped.

Adding further complications to the millionaire's later life, the State of California launched a lawsuit against Whittell, claiming that he spent most of his time in the Golden State as opposed to tax-free Nevada. California demanded state income taxes for previous years, arguing that he had lived at Woodside rather than Lake Tahoe. As Whittell spent only his summers in the Silver State, the elderly tycoon lost the case in 1964, but the state Supreme Court eventually reversed the ruling in Whittell's favor.[12]

At the same time the State of Nevada's case progressed through the courts. Finally, judicial action forced Whittell to sell 5,300 acres for $3,000,000.[13] The

Papers throughout California and Nevada reported Whittell's passing in April 1969. (Courtesy of the San Francisco Chronicle Archives)

loss was an ignoble final chapter for the former playboy who once traveled the world cutting a broad swath. With failing health and decreased mobility, the eighty-seven-year-old George Whittell died on April 18, 1969. When he heard about Whittell's death, Paul Laxalt, by then Nevada's governor, commented, "The State of Nevada is greatly indebted to Captain George Whittell. ...Largely through his efforts, much of Nevada's portion of Lake Tahoe is now preserved. His generosity to the University of Nevada and others will always be remembered."[14]

There was a private funeral in Redwood City near the Captain's Woodside estate. A public memorial service at Whittell High School at Zephyr Cove, Nevada, allowed others to recognize his passing. The remains of George Whittell rest in the family crypt at Cypress Lawn Memorial Park in Colma, California. Flamboyant to the end, Whittell requested that he be buried in his fur coat.

Animals were a cornerstone of the Captain's life, but Bill the lion was always a special friend. Opposite Page: In his isolation, an older Whittell found consolation in nature, such as during this trip to Crater Lake, Oregon.

Whittell had always wrapped himself in folklore, preferring to live within the cocoon of myth away from public scrutiny. With his death, the folklore thrived more than ever, encapsulating the man as if within a drop of amber. It was still possible to see Whittell, but now one had to peer through the murky lens of legend. Only his last will and testament offered a concrete statement revealing the essence of the man. The Captain prefaced the document with the following declaration: "It is my desire the funds be used to relieve pain and suffering among animal, bird and fish life and to preserve, improve and perpetuate animal, bird and fish life...."[15] After leaving $100,000 to the University of San Francisco and establishing trust funds for his wife (who died in 1977) and for his nurse, Ruth Casey, Whittell donated the bulk of his estate to the Defenders of Wildlife, the Society for the Prevention of Cruelty to Animals, and the National Audubon Society. Unfortunately, he did not indicate whether he wanted local or national chapters to receive the proceeds of his good will, and the various levels of the organizations sued one another for the wealth. After years of court action and lawyers' fees, a compromise finally settled the dispute.[16]

Because the Captain did not develop his part of the Tahoe Basin for three crucial decades of regional growth, vast amounts of pristine forest became

A life-long fascination with animals inspired the Captain to leave the majority of his estate to animal rights organizations.

available at a time when attitudes shifted to conservation. In 1970, the U.S. Forest Service obtained 4,732 acres of the Whittell Estate for $1,500,000. Wall Street investor Jack Dreyfus, Jr., purchased most of what remained of the Tahoe property including the Lodge in 1972. The door for preservation of the undeveloped land, however, remained open. In that same year, Dreyfus sold 10,000 acres of his new acquisition to the Forest Service. With this act, the Forest Service completed a period of a dozen-odd years when donations, court-imposed sales, and direct purchases transformed private holdings of valuable Tahoe Basin property into public land, preserved for all time. None of that would have been possible without George Whittell's initial purchase and subsequent reluctance to support development.[17]

Above Right: Elia Whittell with one of her pet cats, an elegant cheetah. Right: Much of the eastern shore of Lake Tahoe retains the pristine nature of this archival photo today, thanks to Whittell's reluctance to sell his land. (Photograph at right courtesy of Liza Casey)

One critical part of the Whittell estate still remained as private property. Dreyfus retained title to the Lodge and a surrounding 140 acres. Regarding these holdings more as investment than residence, he rarely spent a night at the place. Even so, Dreyfus was hardly passive towards the property. The financial mogul paid for a massive addition to the original mansion, hiring Reno-based architect Steve Sederquist to design an annex with sensitivity to the original DeLongchamps plan. ✾

Architect Steve Sederquist designed an addition to the Thunderbird Lodge for its new owner, Jack Dreyfus. He used the existing lighthouse (above left & opposite left) and garage (left & opposite far right) to serve as platforms for his construction, shown in process (upper right & opposite lower left).

Sederquist's addition was attached to the main lodge with a causeway that minimized the intrusion. In response to the requirements of the Tahoe Regional Planning Agency, the nation's first Congressionally created bi-state compact, the new structure did not enlarge the footprint of Whittell's complex. Instead, it rests on the original porch of the Lodge and on the top of the garage, the two wings attached by a hallway that spans a driveway.

Opposite Page & Right:
The Dreyfus Great Room, situated above the lighthouse garage, grows over the Lake. (Courtesy of Scott Klette)

With a nod towards preservation, the new Dreyfus great room, with its stunning views of Lake Tahoe, incorporates Whittell's original lighthouse. Sederquist, working with the Nevada State Historic Preservation Office, attempted to make his 10,000-square-foot addition as compatible as possible. The newer construction more than doubles the size of the main lodge, yet nearly all of the original DeLongchamps buildings remain intact.[18]

The Dreyfus great room rests on the historic garage and incorporates the original lighthouse. The modern room stands in contrast to the smaller dark spaces that for decades had given the Thunderbird Lodge the feeling of a mountain retreat. (Courtesy of Ron James)

In spite of the sensitivity of the architect, the alterations affected the feel of the historic resource. Workers discarded the original wooden floorboards when they buckled after the roof leaked. In addition, in the early 1980s, skylights were added to brighten the main hall, modernizing its atmosphere from that of a brooding hunting lodge to an airier mountain resort. The change damaged the structural integrity of the roof and the historic significance of a magical place. 🌿

By the 1990s, Dreyfus decided it was time to cash in on his investment. He placed the Lodge and his remaining acreage on the market. The fate of this prime real estate was in the balance. It could be the site of environmentally destructive development or its preservation could add to the quality of the Lake and the Tahoe Basin. Dreyfus wanted to realize a profit but was willing to consider a plan to move the estate into public hands. Extended negotiations between organizations and public agencies took years, and many times failure seemed imminent. Ultimately, an assortment of governmental agencies, non-profit organizations, and a private corporation arrived at a solution. 🌿

This Page & Opposite Page: The stunning elegance of the Lodge's 1938 great room has inspired awe for decades. (Photograph opposite page courtesy of Scott Klette)

In a complicated land exchange, Del Webb Corporation purchased Las Vegas real estate managed by the Bureau of Land Management. Proceeds from the sale were then used to buy most of the Dreyfus acreage for the U.S. Forest Service. Unfortunately, the land exchange could not be used to acquire the Lodge itself. With the help of the American Land Conservancy, an environmentally minded nonprofit corporation, and Nevada's U.S. Senators Harry Reid and Richard Bryan, an intricate arrangement agreeable to all parties finally emerged. A new nonprofit organization called the Thunderbird Lodge Preservation Society would assume the mortgage held by Del Webb Corporation. The University of Nevada, Reno, also participated by assuring maintenance and scientific use of the property as a research station. Finally, on October 15, 1999, the land transfer was complete and the Preservation Society took over management responsibilities of Whittell's complex of buildings.[19]

Thanks to the efforts of many dedicated people, Whittell's environmental and architectural legacy endures. From the gatehouse (above) to the main lodge, (right & opposite) before the addition of ornamental iron details, the diverse historic district presents many preservation challenges.

The mission of the Thunderbird Lodge Preservation Society is to promote, for charitable and educational purposes, the preservation of the Thunderbird Lodge. The Society emphasizes the public appreciation of art and design by celebrating the architectural structure, plan, and the cultural significance of the Thunderbird Lodge and grounds.

Since the acquisition of the site, the non-profit organization has made considerable progress as it repairs deteriorated masonry and reverses many non-historic alterations. Restoration work in 2004 removed the Dreyfus kitchen in the main lodge. The historic bar, which had languished in storage, returned to its home. Careful hands removed the milky wash from the wood, revealing the original red coloring accented by a delicate green cast. The following year, craftsmen removed the skylights, and repaired the truss system, which the Dreyfus alteration had weakened. Finally, the historic great room returned to its original grandeur.

Recent resotration work, shown top left in progress, removed the skylights from the ceiling & replaced boards with hand-hewn wood to match the original (top middle & right). Tedious paint removal lifted the Dreyfus milky wash from the wood, a process shown in progress (above & right). (Courtesy of Ron James)

Opposite Page: Dreyfus put Whittell's bar into storage, shown opposite above, but the Thunderbird Lodge Preservation Society removed the Dreyfus kitchen and restored the historic bar, as shown opposite left & right. (Opposite bottom left & right courtesy of Ron James)

The University of Nevada, Reno, played a crucial role during the land transfers and acquisitions, providing the Preservation Society with much-needed credibility that convinced decision-makers to proceed with the plan. Since that time, the University has stepped away from the property as the Thunderbird Lodge Preservation Society creates its own future, serving the public through tours and a wide variety of programming.

There are many challenges facing the Preservation Society in the new century. Fund-raising to eliminate the mortgage is a primary concern. In addition, the historic masonry that covers acres in the form of buildings, paths, stairs, lighthouses, tunnels, and the lagoon, needs repairs and ongoing maintenance. The Society is also working to create programs that best serve visitors and the community.

Left & Opposite Page: The Thunderbird Lodge Preservation Society maintains Whittell's estate for the public benefit. The Society hosts dozens of events every year for popular enjoyment. (Courtesy of Vance Fox)

In all, the Thunderbird Lodge Preservation Society has a huge responsibility to care for the property and to make certain that it remains a valued part of Lake Tahoe and the nation. Through accidents of history and his personal commitment to avoid work, George Whittell's involvement preserved thousands of acres of forest, enhancing the quality of the Lake Tahoe ecosystem and its aesthetic value. In addition, his Thunderbird property is one of the region's most remarkable historic sites. Fortunately, history has been kind to this resource. Acquisition by the Preservation Society begins a new chapter for Whittell's legacy. Working for the public benefit, the non-profit organization must now ensure that the future is equally benevolent.

The Captain did not like neighbors and refused to develop his side of Lake Tahoe. Today, his former estate includes a pristine coast and the historic lodge and its grounds. (Courtesy of Ron James)

Chapter 3 Notes

[1] Fr. Don Mason, letter dated March 14, 1985, TLPS Archive.

[2] Barney and Dohrmann, "Interview with Warren Crane."

[3] Recollection of John Lewis, relayed on History Day at the Thunderbird Lodge, September 3, 2000. Lewis had conducted a great deal of research into the Whittell family. "One Dead, Five Hurt in Lake Tahoe Crash." *Nevada State Journal* (September 2, 1954); "Crash Victim's Funeral is Held." *Nevada State Journal* (September 3, 1954); "Tahoe Woman Dies in Wreck at Crystal Bay." *Reno Evening Gazette* (September 2, 1954); Fr. Don Mason, letter dated March 14, 1985, TLPS Archive.

[4] Phil Caterino, former Director of the TLPS, indicated a former caretaker had told him the story of the loud funeral dirges disturbing Lake residents. Interview June 13, 2001. Barney and Dohrmann, "Interview with Warren Crane."

[5] Barney and Dohrmann, "Interview with Warren Crane." See also *San Francisco Chronicle* (September 19, 1989) B5. The X-ray of Whittell's leg is on file in the TLPS Archive.

[6] Recollection of John Lewis, relayed on History Day at the Thunderbird Lodge, September 3, 2000; Barney and Dohrmann, "Interview with Warren Crane."

[7] Laxalt, *Nevada's Paul Laxalt*, 74-78.

[8] Much of this summary represents the point of view expressed by John Lewis, relayed on History Day at the Thunderbird Lodge, September 3, 2000.

[9] Laxalt, *Nevada's Paul Laxalt*, 74-78; "Whittell Gives U.N. Sierra Valley." *Nevada State Journal* (December 31, 1959); "University of Nevada Seventieth Annual Commencement." June 5-6, 1960, program available at the University Archives, Department of Special Collections, University of Nevada, Reno Library; Letter to Whittell from William Wood, President, University of Nevada, June 16, 1958, TLPS Archive.

[10] Grant Sawyer, *Hang Tough! Grant Sawyer, an Activist in the Governor's Mansion: from Oral History Interviews with Grant Sawyer.* (Reno, Nevada: University of Nevada Press, 1993); "Court Ruling on Whittell's Tahoe Land." *San Francisco Chronicle* (October 5, 1965); letters dated November 27, 1961 to "Captain George Whittell" and to "Mrs. George Whittell," Sawyer File, State Archives, Nevada State Library and Archives, Department of Cultural Affairs; recollection of John Lewis, relayed on History Day at the Thunderbird Lodge, September 3, 2000; "Whittell Land Set for E. Tahoe Park." *San Francisco Sunday Examiner and Chronicle* (November 19, 1967); "At Last...A Park for Lake Tahoe." *Nevada Highways and Parks*, Spring 1965, 4-15, 58.

[11] Strong, *Tahoe*, 54-55, 128-129, 196; TLPS Archive includes numerous documents related to land sales and proposed land sales in the 1960s; "Option Taken by Investors on Property." *Nevada State Journal* (September 9, 1959); "Oppose Gaming in State Park." *Nevada State Journal* (April 14, 1962).

[12] "Tax Fight Won by Millionaire." *San Francisco Chronicle* (May 17, 1963); "He's a Californian – For Taxes." *San Francisco Chronicle* (December 18, 1964).

[13] *San Francisco Chronicle*, (November 19, 1967) 3; Strong, *Tahoe*, 64, 90.

[14] "Sportsman George Whittell Dies at 87." *Reno Evening Gazette* (April 19, 1969); "George B. Whittell Succumbs at 87." *San Francisco Chronicle* (April 19, 1969); "George Whittell, Financier, Dies." *Nevada State Journal* (April 19, 1969); "Funeral Rites Today for George Whittell." *Tahoe Daily Tribune* (April 21, 1969).

[15] George Whittell, Jr., Last Will and Testament, available at Department of Special Collections, University of Nevada, Reno Library; "Whittell Wealth Goes to Wildlife." *Nevada State Journal* (June 7, 1969).

[16] For Elia's death see "Mrs. Whittell Dies in Paris." Clipping without provenience available at the TLPS Archive; "Whittell's Influence on Tahoe Recalled." *Lake Tahoe Bonanza* (June 1, 1977); for the protracted lawsuit over Whittell's estate, see Fenster, "The Private Universe of George Whittell," 105; Recollection of John Lewis, relayed on History Day at the Thunderbird Lodge, September 3, 2000.

[17] Strong, *Tahoe*, 83, 93; see also Jack Dreyfus, *The Lion of Wall Street.* (Washington, D.C.: Regency Publishing, 1996).

[18] The TLPS Archive and the Nevada State Historic Preservation Office in the Department of Cultural Affairs have documents related to the Dreyfus acquisition and addition.

[19] The TLPS Archive and the Nevada State Historic Preservation Office have documents related to the acquisition of the Dreyfus-Whittell property in 1999.

Opposite Page: The fountain at the Thunderbird Lodge remains from the days when water encircled Whittell mansion. (Courtesy of Scott Klette

RONALD M. JAMES is Nevada's State Historic Preservation Officer. He is the author of four other books, including *The Roar and the Silence: A History of Virginia City and the Comstock Lode*, winner of the Shepperson Humanities award for 1998. James is a historian and folklorist whose publications deal with European and American topics.

SUSAN A. JAMES is a historian who has taught at the University of Nevada, Reno. Her publications have appeared in popular magazines treating a wide variety of Nevada-related topics. She has curated museum exhibits and served as a Scholar-in-Residence for the Nevada Humanities Committee.